EFFECTIVE WORK BREAKDOWN STRUCTURES

The books in the Project Management Essential Library series provide project managers with new skills and innovative approaches to the fundamentals of effectively managing projects.

Additional titles in the series include:

Managing Projects for Value, John C. Goodpasture

Project Planning and Scheduling, Gregory T. Haugan

Managing Project Quality, Timothy J. Kloppenborg and Joseph A. Petrick

Project Measurement, Steve Neuendorf

Project Estimating and Cost Management, Parviz F. Rad

Project Risk Management: A Proactive Approach, Paul S. Royer

MANAGEMENTCONCEPTS
www.managementconcepts.com

EFFECTIVE WORK BREAKDOWN STRUCTURES

Gregory T. Haugan

𝗠 MANAGEMENTCONCEPTS

Vienna, Virginia

𝄽𝄽
MANAGEMENTCONCEPTS
8230 Leesburg Pike, Suite 800
Vienna, VA 22182
(703) 790-9595
Fax: (703) 790-1371
www.managementconcepts.com

Printed in the United States of America

Library of Congress Cataloging-in-Publication Data

Haugan, Gregory T., 1931–
    Effective work breakdown structures/Gregory T. Haugan.
        p. cm. — (Project management essential library series)
    Includes bibliographical references and index.
    ISBN 978-1-56726-135-6 (pbk.) ⌐
    1. Project management. I. Title. II. Project management essential library.
HD69.P75 II377 2001
658.4'04—dc21

                                                    2001044668

About the Author

Gregory T. Haugan, Ph.D., PMP, has been a Vice President with GLH Incorporated for the past 16 years, specializing in project management consulting and training. He has more than 40 years of experience as a consultant and as a government and private sector official in the planning, scheduling, management, and operation of projects of all sizes, as well as in the development and implementation of project management and information systems.

Dr. Haugan is an expert in the application and implementation of project management systems. He participated in the early development of WBS and C/SCS (earned value) concepts at DoD and in the initial development of PERT cost software. He was the Martin Marietta representative on the Joint Army Navy NASA Committee developing the initial C/SCS concepts. He is particularly expert in the areas of scope management, cost management and schedule management, setting up new projects, and preparing proposals.

Dr. Haugan received his Ph.D. from the American University, his MBA from St. Louis University, and his BSME from the Illinois Institute of Technology.

I dedicate this book
to
my wife Susan,
for her love and support

Table of Contents

Foreword

One of the most significant contributions to management theory and practice has been the development of the field of project management, which evolved from work in the 1960s by the Department of Defense, the aerospace industry, and the construction industry. Many different tools to assist project managers resulted from these early efforts. These tools, which include the work breakdown structure (WBS) network planning algorithms known as PERT, CPM, and PDM, and project management software, have significantly improved the ability to develop effective plans and schedules, which is essential for excellence in project management.

Dr. Gregory T. Haugan participated actively from the beginning in the development of project management. Dr. Haugan was the Martin Marietta representative to the DoD/NASA PERT/cost working group in the early 1960s, when the body of knowledge in project management began to be documented. Work by this group subsequently led to the U.S. Air Force publication in 1963 of a PERT/cost system description manual that included a section identifying the WBS as one of the key concepts for successful project management.

Dr. Haugan also was co-chairman and one of the speakers at an American Management Association program on PERT/cost in 1964. This meeting was one of the first in which a WBS was developed and was discussed as being instrumental for effective project management.

Since projects are managed to meet stated requirements, successful project management requires starting the project on the correct path. Developing a comprehensive WBS to serve as the framework for the entire project is the only way to do this. In concept this is easy, but in practice it is more difficult because project managers and planners do not approach the concept with a full understanding of the WBS, the discipline required, and how to develop and use it. In fact, many are not even aware of the principles involved.

This timely book provides comprehensive insights into the development and application of the WBS, as well as the details of the WBS and principles for its use. Dr. Haugan's many years of practical experience make him eminently qualified to write such a book, and when reading it, you will see that he practices what he preaches.

Dr. Haugan presents several new concepts regarding different types of WBS structures for projects involving new product development, services, and results, and different types of WBS elements designed to describe different types of work.

This book is important for project managers and planners who wish to get their projects started right and need to know how best to proceed. I am confident you will benefit from reading it, and it will serve as a critical reference and guidebook for your future work in project management.

Dr. Ginger Levin

Preface

This book is intended to fill a long-standing need for a comprehensive, cohesive, and practical description of the work breakdown structure (WBS) concept and its application. It is designed for the project manager or project planner to help improve the structuring of the project as an important step toward getting the project started effectively and to use the WBS throughout the life of the project as a key tool for planning, control, and communication.

The book represents many years of experience in the development of work breakdown structures and in the scoping and planning of new projects. The book presents the generally accepted concepts of the use and application of the WBS, although many of the more detailed concepts are mine. Many examples are provided.

The WBS is not a new concept in project management, but it is often misunderstood and not used as it should be for maximum effectiveness. The use of the WBS requires discipline and thought, like any planning. It always seems easier to just start doing the work rather than to plan the work you are going to do.

This book is organized into six chapters:

- **Chapter 1** serves as the **Introduction**, defining the subject, presenting a brief history of the WBS concept, defining terms, and identifying the role of the WBS concept in the project management process.
- **Chapter 2, Work Breakdown Structure Fundamentals**, discusses various aspects of and considerations in the development of an effective WBS.
- **Chapter 3, Lifecycle Planning: Programs and Phases**, presents the concept that each lifecycle phase is a project with its own WBS.
- **Chapter 4, The WBS in Project Operations**, presents the relationship to and use of the WBS in each of the nine *PMBOK® Guide* areas.[1]

---

[1] *PMBOK® Guide* is a trademark of the Project Management Institute, Inc. which is registered in the United States and other nations.

- **Chapter 5, WBS Examples and Descriptions,** includes examples of the WBS for several different types of projects and how the fundamentals presented in Chapter 2 apply universally.
- **Chapter 6, WBS Principles, Steps, and Checklist,** includes a summary of WBS principles and a list of specific, pragmatic steps recommended for the project manager to develop the project WBS.

This book is a product of my 40 years of project management experience, including participating as the Martin Company (currently Lockheed Martin) representative to a government-industry task force in the 1960s when many of the project management tools now in daily use throughout the world were first developed. As a project manager, a consultant to project managers, and a trainer and course developer, I have been involved in the development of hundreds of WBSs, and much of this experience is reflected in this book.

Thanks goes to Cathy Kreyche of Management Concepts, Inc., and my business partner, Dr. Ginger Levin, who encouraged me in this endeavor and provided many useful editorial and substantive comments.

Gregory T. Haugan

CHAPTER 1

Introduction to the Work Breakdown Structure

This introductory chapter provides information on the work breakdown structure (WBS), the background of the concept, and its place in the project management process.

THE PROJECT PROBLEM AND SOLUTION

Starting a new project is like starting to write a book—you have an idea of what you want to do, but are not sure how to start. Many writers, like many project planners and managers, find that outlining is frequently the most effective way to start writing.[1]

An outline is both a method for organizing material and a plan for the book itself. There are many ways to outline a book, especially one based on research. In general, it is necessary to plan the research or data gathering, and decide what will be discussed in each chapter and the appendices. In addition, it is necessary to take into account drafting chapters, getting critical reviews from other experts, and the actual steps involved in reviewing proofs and publishing the document. A sample outline is included in the form of a WBS in Chapter 5.

A frequently used analogy is the old question: "How do you eat an elephant?" The answer, of course, is: "One bite at a time." So the first step in preparing an outline is to start defining and categorizing the "bites." The bites are important because that is where the useful work is accomplished. For a project, brainstorming can help define the "bites" or activities from the bottom up or a process of "decomposition" can be used starting from the top, and subdividing the project (or the entire elephant) into major sections and working down as shown in Figure 1-1. In either approach, the objective is to develop a structure of the work that needs to be done for the project.

It is obvious that the parts of the elephant can be broken down (or subdivided) further. For example, the head is made up of a face, ears, tusks, and trunk; the four legs can be individually identified; body parts identified, and the tail and tuft separated. A WBS for a project follows the same concept.

FIGURE 1-1   Elephant Breakdown Structure

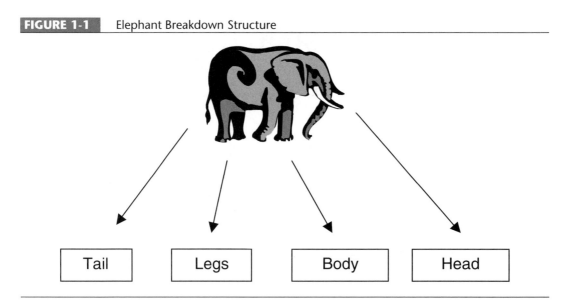

| Tail | Legs | Body | Head |

The WBS is an outline of the work; it is not the work itself. The work is the sum of many activities that make up the project.

A WBS may start either as an informal list of activities or in a very structured way, depending on the project and the constraints, and it can end wherever the planner wants it to. The goal is to have a useful framework to help define and organize the work and then to get started doing it.

In developing an outline for a book, for example, some things happen almost automatically, growing out of the discipline of the process. First, boundaries need to be imposed on the book's contents. Preparing an outline forces the author to define the topics, parts, sections, and chapters. The same thing happens when the project's WBS is developed. Assumptions and constraints are often considered without focusing on them directly.

Developing the WBS is a four-step process:

1. Specifying the project objectives and focusing on the products, services, or results to be provided to the customer
2. Identifying specifically the products, services, or results (deliverables or end items) to be provided to the customer
3. Identifying other work areas in the project to make sure that 100 percent of the work is covered and to identify areas that cut across the deliverables, represent intermediate outputs, or complement the deliverables.
4. Subdividing each of the items in steps 2 and 3 into successive, logical subcategories until the complexity and dollar value of the elements

KEY DEFINITIONS

Most of the project management terms used frequently in this book are in common usage in the project management field. The following definitions are included in the Glossary of the Project Management Institute's *A Guide to the Project Management Book of Knowledge*, known as the *PMBOK® Guide*.[2]

Activity: An element of work performed during the course of a project that includes a verb in its descriptor signifying action. An activity normally has an expected duration, expected cost, and expected resource requirements. Activities are often subdivided into tasks.[3]

Deliverable: Any measurable, tangible, verifiable outcome, result, or item that must be produced to complete a project or part of a project. Often used more narrowly in reference to an external deliverable, which is a deliverable that is subject to approval by the project sponsor or customer.

End Item: A general term that represents the hardware, services, equipment, facilities, data, etc., that are deliverable to the customer or that constitute a commitment on the part of the project manager to the customer.

Organizational Breakdown Structure (OBS): A depiction of the project organization arranged so as to relate work packages to organizational units.

Program: A group of related projects managed in a coordinated way. Programs usually include an element of ongoing work.

Project: A temporary endeavor undertaken to create a unique product, service, or result.

Responsibility Assignment Matrix (RAM): A structure that relates the project organization structure to the WBS to help ensure that each element of the project scope of work is assigned to a responsible individual.

Subproject: A smaller portion of the overall project according to the *PMBOK® Guide*. Usually, a subproject is a WBS element that can be managed as a semi-independent element of the project and is the responsibility of one person or organization.

Task: A generic term for work that is not included in the WBS, but potentially could be a further decomposition of work by the individuals responsible for that work. Also used to describe the lowest level of effort on a project.

WBS Dictionary: A document that describes the work performed in each WBS element.

WBS Element: An entry in the WBS that can be at any level and is described by a noun or noun and adjective.

Work Breakdown Structure (WBS): A deliverable-oriented grouping of project elements that organizes and defines the total work scope of the project. Each descending level represents an increasingly detailed definition of the project work.

Work Package: The lowest level work element in the WBS that provides a logical basis for defining activities or assigning responsibility to a specific person or organization. Also, the work required to complete a specific job or process such as a report, a design, a documentation requirement or portion thereof, a piece of hardware or a service.[4]

become manageable units for planning and control purposes (work packages).

In the early phases of a project, it may be feasible to develop only a two- to three-level WBS, since the details of the work may yet be undefined. However, as the project progresses into the project definition phase or planning phase, the planning becomes more detailed. The subdivisions of the WBS can be developed to successively lower levels at that time. These final subcategories or work packages are the "bites" that we are going to use to "eat the elephant" or to perform the project work. The product of this subcategorization process is the completed WBS.

For example, in a project to build a new garage for our new car, the steps are as follows:

- **Step 1. Specify the project objectives:** build a one-car garage with landscaping on the existing lot; the garage should have internal and external lighting and plumbing for water.
- **Step 2. Identify specifically the products, services, or results (deliverables or end items):** the garage and the landscaped grounds.
- **Step 3. Identify other work areas to make sure that 100 percent of the work is identified:** A project management function is needed to do such things as construction planning, obtaining permits, and awarding subcontracts.

    The WBS so far would look like that shown in Figure 1-2. Level 1 is the total project and Level 2 is the subdivision into the final products (a garage and landscaped grounds) plus cross-cutting or complementary work needed for the project (such as project management). The project's total scope is represented by the work as the sum of the three Level 2 elements.
- **Step 4. Subdivide the elements until a level is achieved that is suitable for planning and control:** The next level subdivision of each Level 2 element is shown in Figure 1-3.

Further breakdown of some of the Level 3 elements can be performed. The complete WBS to the work package level, which is adequate for planning and control, is shown in Figure 1-4. In this figure, the WBS is presented in outline format rather than the space-consuming graphic format used previously. Either format is acceptable. The outline format is generally used when entering WBS data into project management software packages or to save space in documents.

At the next level below the work packages are the individual tasks or activities. These are not normally considered a part of the WBS. In fact (as discussed in Chapter 2), one of the primary uses of the WBS is to provide a framework to assist in defining the activities of the project. When the WBS is complete, it covers the total scope of the project.

This brings up a very important project management principle: Work not included in the WBS is outside the scope of the project. For example,

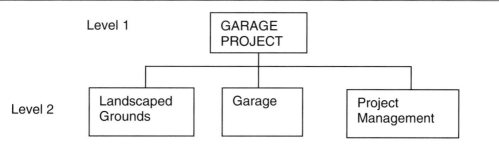

FIGURE 1-2 Top-Level Work Breakdown Structure

in Figure 1-4, there is no heating, ventilating, and air conditioning (HVAC) system shown; therefore, an HVAC system is not part of the project.

Once the WBS is established, it must be maintained and updated to reflect changes in the project. The configuration and content of the WBS and the specific work packages vary from project to project depending upon several considerations:

- Size and complexity of the project
- Structure of the organizations involved
- Phase of the project
- Project manager judgment of work allocations to subcontractors
- Degree of uncertainty and risk involved
- Time available for planning.

The WBS is a marvelous communication tool to present the project's scope in an understandable form and to coordinate this understanding within the project team and between the project team and other stakeholders. At the

FIGURE 1-3 WBS to Level 3

Level 1		GARAGE PROJECT	
Level 2	Landscaped Grounds	Garage	Project Management
Level 3	• Driveway • Landscaping	• Materials • Foundation • Walls • Roof • Utilities	• Construction Planning • Permits • Inspections • Subcontracts

FIGURE 1-4   Garage Project Work Breakdown Structure

LEVEL 1	LEVEL 2	LEVEL 3	LEVEL 4
Garage Project	Landscaped Grounds	Driveway	
		Landscaping	
	Garage	Materials	
		Foundation	
		Walls	Walls and Siding
			Windows
			Garage Door
			Service Door
			Assembly
		Roof	Trusses
			Covering
			Gutters and Drains
		Utilities	Electrical
			Plumbing
	Project Management	Construction Planning	
		Permits	
		Inspections	
		Financing	
		Subcontracts	

end of the planning phase, the plans and schedules are frozen or "baselined" and become the basis for executing the work of the project. At the same time, the WBS is baselined and becomes one of the key mechanisms for change management. Work that is proposed that is not in the WBS needs to be added to the project and to the WBS through formal change control processes.

The following charts show two additional sample WBSs. They focus on the output products or deliverables of the project. Figure 1-5 is a sample WBS for a civilian aircraft project in which a passenger aircraft is to be converted into a freighter. The output products are a certified-airworthy converted aircraft, technical manuals, and a list of spare part requirements.

This WBS contains a cross-cutting set of work activities labeled "system engineering" that encompasses the work necessary to define the conversion. This is a common type of WBS element.

The second sample, Figure 1-6, is a software development project; the primary deliverable is the software system and the secondary deliverables are the training materials and the user documents. The software system also has a cross-cutting set of work activities labeled "system analyses" that represents work such as project definition and workflow analyses or structured analyses.

The WBS can be used, in whole or in part, to make assignments, issue budgets, and explain the scope and nature of a project. Responsibilities are assigned at the lowest level—the work package level—or the next level—the task or activity level. The WBS serves as a common focal point for presenting the totality of a project.

BACKGROUND OF THE WBS CONCEPT

The WBS is not a new concept in project management and some background will assist in understanding its important role.

Early U.S. Government Activities

In 1959, Malcolm, Roseboom, Clark, and Fazar published a classic paper describing the successful implementation of a technique called "Program Evaluation and Review Technique," or PERT.[5] Although the work breakdown structure is not addressed directly, the graphics include a breakdown in illustrating how this concept was evolving (see Figure 1-7).

The PERT and WBS concepts spread widely and swiftly. These management systems and their application, as developed between 1958 and 1965,

FIGURE 1-5   Sample WBS—Aircraft Conversion Project

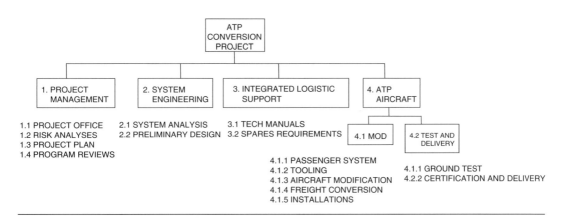

FIGURE 1-6  Sample WBS—Software Project

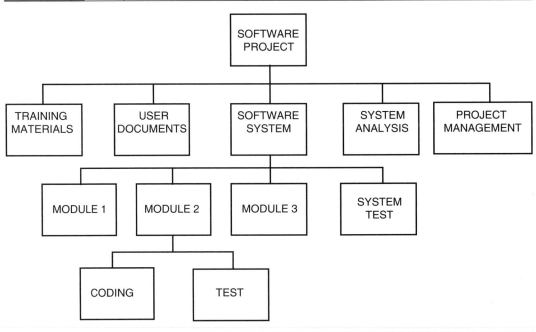

are the basis for much of the project management body of knowledge used today. By 1961, the term *work breakdown structure* was in common use. A sample of a WBS was included in an article published within General Electric Corporation.[6] Part of this WBS was for the Fleet Ballistic Missile Maintenance Training Facility, shown in Figure 1-8.

The output products include modification of government-furnished equipment, other equipment, documentation, trainers, and simulators. The

FIGURE 1-7 Early Polaris Project Work Subsystems

Fleet Ballistic Missile Program Subsystems	
Missile	Re-Entry Body Guidance Ballistic Shell Propulsion Flight Controls
Launcher	
Navigation	
Fire Control	
Ships	
Command Communications	

FIGURE 1-8   Work Breakdown Structure—1961

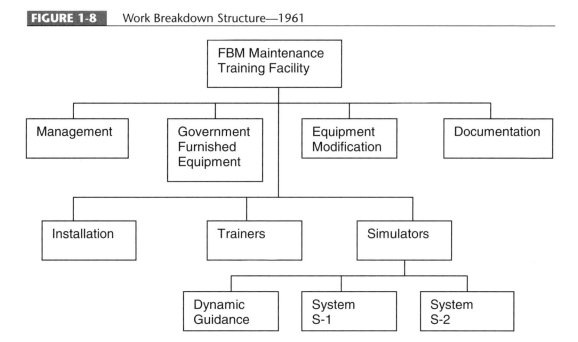

other elements of management and installation are cross-cutting or support elements.

In June 1962, the Department of Defense (DoD), in cooperation with the National Aeronautics and Space Administration (NASA) and the aerospace industry, published a document intended to guide the systems design of the PERT Cost system.[7] This document included an extensive description of the WBS that is essentially the same as used today.[8]

In October 1962, NASA published another document that expanded on the discussion of the WBS in the *NASA DoD Guide to PERT Cost*.[9] NASA stresses that a top-down approach is used in the development of the WBS to ensure that the total project is fully planned and the derivative plans contribute directly to end objectives. Also, that in any integrated time/cost management system, it is imperative that both cost and time are planned and controlled from a common framework.

Within the aerospace industry, the various companies were rapidly incorporating the concept of the WBS into their internal project planning operations. The author was using the WBS in his planning in the Baltimore Division and the Orlando Division of Martin Marietta (now Lockheed Martin), and published a document that included the required development of a WBS in its project planning when using PERT.[10]

In August 1964, the U.S. government published the *PERT Implementation Manual*, which included a discussion of the WBS.[11] This document was intended for use by any government agency or private or public institution. In this document, a top-down approach to developing the WBS also is espoused so that "detailed plans will not be developed outside a common framework."[12] The authors stated that plans, schedules, and network plans can be developed without a WBS, but such plans and schedules are likely to be incomplete or inconsistent with project objectives and output products.

The development of a WBS in all government and aerospace industry documents typically follows the same pattern. The planning begins at the highest level of the project with identification of objectives and end items. When developing the WBSs for large military systems such as those that existed in the 1960s, it became apparent that the top two or three levels were very similar for each family of systems; that is, the end items and the next level decomposition of the end items were the same. For example, all aircraft have wings, engines, a fuselage, empennage, landing gear, etc., regardless of whether they are transports, fighters, or bombers.

In 1968, DoD developed a standard for the top-level decomposition of work breakdown structures for DoD systems.[13] This document was made mandatory for application to all defense projects estimated to exceed $10 million using research, development, test, and engineering funds. On January 2, 1998, MIL-HDBK-881 updated and superseded the MIL-STD-881 documents. Because of a change in DoD philosophy, the handbook cannot be cited as a contractual obligation. However, other DoD documents specifically require a WBS.[14]

MIL-HDBK-881 is still directed at defense materiel items. The WBS templates for the same seven DoD systems that were in the original standard are still included in the handbook. The handbook includes the top three levels of the WBS and the associated descriptions (WBS dictionary) for the following systems:

1. Aircraft systems
2. Electronic/automated software systems
3. Missile systems
4. Ordnance systems
5. Ship systems
6. Space systems
7. Surface vehicle systems.

Figure 1-9 presents the ship system WBS as included in the handbook.[15]

The levels below those described in the handbook are usually defined by the contractor and are unique to each project. It is not unusual for five to eight additional levels to be identified in these types of large systems.

The Project Management Institute and the *PMBOK® Guide*

The lead in monitoring and documenting project management practices transitioned from the public to the private sector with the reductions in the

FIGURE 1-9   Ship System WBS

Level 1	Level 2	Level 3
Ship System	Ship	Hull Structure
		Propulsion Plant
		Electric Plant
		Command and Surveillance
		Auxiliary Systems
		Outfit and Furnishings
		Armament
		Integration/Engineering
		Ship Assembly and Support Services
	Systems Engineering/ Program Management	Development Test and Evaluation
		Operational Test and Evaluation
		Mockups
	System Test and Evaluation	Test and Evaluation Support
		Test Facilities
	Training	Equipment
		Services
		Facilities
	Data	Technical Publications
		Engineering Data
		Management Data
		Support Data
		Data Depository
	Peculiar Support Equipment	Test and Measurement Equipment
		Support and Handling Equipment
	Common Support Equipment	Test and Measurement Equipment
		Support and Handling Equipment
	Operational/Site Activation	System Assembly, Installation and Checkout on Site
		Contractor Technical Support
		Site Construction
		Site/Ship/Vehicle Conversion
	Industrial Facilities	Construction/Conversion/Expansion
		Equipment Acquisition or Modernization
		Maintenance (Industrial Facilities)
	Initial Spares and Repair Parts	

Source: Department of Defense, MIL-STD-881 *Work Breakdown Structures for Defense Materiel Items* (Washington D.C.: Headquarters, Air Force Systems Command, Directorate of Cost Analysis, 1 November 1968).

space program, the end of the cold war, and the rapid growth of the Project Management Institute (PMI®).

The Role of the Project Management Institute

PMI®, a professional association of over 70,000 members, through its conferences, chapter meetings, the monthly magazine *PM Network*,[®][16] and the quarterly *Project Management Journal*,[®][17] provides a forum for the growth and development of project management practices. In August 1987, PMI® published a landmark document entitled *The Project Management Body of Knowledge*. This document was revised, entitled *A Guide to the Project Management Body of Knowledge*, republished in 1996, and updated in 2000.

The *PMBOK® Guide* reflects the 30 years of experience gained in project management since the seminal work of DoD, NASA, other government organizations, and the aerospace industry in the 1960s.

The **PMBOK®** Guide

The *PMBOK® Guide* includes widely applied, proven, traditional practices as well as knowledge of innovative and advanced practices that have more limited use but are generally accepted.

The *PMBOK® Guide* is not intended as a "how to" document, but instead provides a structured overview and basic reference to the concepts of the profession of project management. The *PMBOK® Guide* focuses on project management processes.

The *PMBOK® Guide* is not as explicit as is the MIL-HDBK-881 and the other U.S. government documents on the development of the WBS. There are some differences, as might be expected with 30 additional years of experience. The *PMBOK® Guide* addresses a broader audience than the DoD documents, including all commercial applications and experience since the 1960s. In addition to the discussion of the WBS in the *PMBOK® Guide*, PMI® is in the process of developing a *Practice Standard for Work Breakdown Structures* that is intended to be more universal in application than the comparable DoD handbook.[18] The *Practice Standard* is scheduled for publication in 2001, and will complement this book in the same manner that the *PMBOK® Guide* complements other books on project management topics.

The *PMBOK® Guide* follows early government experience in the area of decomposition, which is described as: "subdividing the major project deliverables or subdeliverables into smaller, more manageable components until the deliverables are defined in sufficient detail to support development of project activities (planning, executing, controlling, and closing)."[19]

The PMBOK® Guide *versus DoD*

On the surface, the primary difference between the *PMBOK® Guide* and the DoD handbook appears to be the philosophy of how decomposition may be accomplished. The *PMBOK® Guide* states: ". . .the major elements should always be defined in terms of how the project will actually be organized."[20] The DoD handbook states: "A WBS should not influence or in any way affect the contractor's program organization."[21] One of the universal principles of developing a WBS is that it is not an organizational chart. The wording in the *PMBOK® Guide* should be interpreted in terms of how the work is organized, not the human resources organization structure.

The *PMBOK® Guide* also uses the example of the phases of the project lifecycle as the first level of decomposition. On the other hand, the DoD handbook states: "Program phases. . .are inappropriate as elements in a work breakdown structure."[22] Also, while the DoD handbook does not permit lifecycle phases to be elements of the WBS, this is a DoD-peculiar restriction and relates to the DoD definition and use of a program WBS. Chapter 3 discusses the use of phases as the program's top level WBS and the differences are reconciled between the *PMBOK® Guide* and the DoD approach.

WBS Element Descriptions

The classical approach to the WBS generally identifies the elements in the WBS as being described by nouns and modifiers. Further, the WBS can be thought of as the response to the question: "*What* has to be accomplished in the project?"[23] The network diagram developed from the definition and relationships of activities answers the question: "*How* will it be accomplished?" and the schedule resulting from the network calculations responds to: "*When* will it be accomplished?"

There have been some recommendations that PMI® accept activity-like descriptions in the WBS that would include verbs. However, the basic traditional approach is sound and proven, and the use of activities—like descriptions in a WBS—should be limited to those cultures where any other approach is unworkable. Activities, by definition, are action entities and include verbs in their descriptors.

This book follows the philosophy that the WBS structure must be related to the objectives of the project and therefore produces the unique product, service, or results as PMI® defines a project. The WBS must be an end-item or deliverable-oriented, and the WBS is preferably composed of elements that can be described by nouns modified by adjectives as necessary for clarity. The reason to prefer this type of description is the discipline of focusing on the output products, which are usually things that are described by nouns. Using verbs implies action, which is ideally performed at the activity level below the lowest level of the WBS.

For the WBS to be fully understandable to persons other than the developer, a separate document defining the content of each element is often needed. (This is called a WBS dictionary and is discussed in Chapter 2). However, by using longer phrases, often including verbs in the element descriptors, the work content of the WBS element can sometimes be described sufficiently to eliminate the need for a WBS dictionary. The project environment and the project itself should determine the nature of the descriptors used for the elements of the WBS. It is necessary to have a set of WBS descriptors that help stakeholders understand the work represented by each element.

One of the primary purposes of the WBS is communication. It is therefore necessary to have a format with which the audience can identify. It is then possible for activities—verb statements—to be included in the WBS. However, it is important that the WBS be based on the deliverables—the output products of the project—regardless of how the elements are described. (See Chapter 2 for the relation of WBS elements to work packages and activities.)

The material in this book follows the *PMBOK® Guide*, or more correctly, the *PMBOK® Guide* reflects the body of knowledge of WBS use addressed herein.

THE WBS IN THE PROJECT MANAGEMENT PROCESS

Managing projects is a continuous process. Figure 1-10 illustrates the basic project management process. It focuses on achieving the project objectives within the project management triad of time-cost-quality (performance) constraints and goals.

Each of the ten steps has a specific output that is defined and documented. The steps are frequently iterative; that is, circumstances arising in accomplishing later steps may require revision of an earlier step and subsequent repetition of all or part of the succeeding steps. This constant iteration and replanning characterize the day-to-day activities of the project manager and the project team.

The basic project management process has five types of activities: initiation, planning, execution, controlling, and closing (see Figure 1-10). This categorization emphasizes the importance of planning before extensive

FIGURE 1-10   Basic Project Management Process

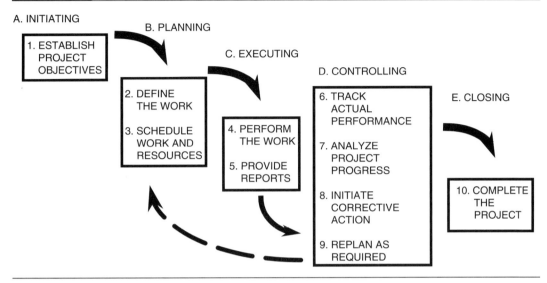

project work begins and the importance of bringing the project to closure once all the work is done.

The WBS is the key tool in the planning phase, where the work is defined, and, at the completion of the planning phase, when the plan—including the WBS—is baselined. Chapter 4 discusses the WBS being omnipresent in virtually every aspect of managing the project. Therefore, it is very important to prepare the WBS early and correctly.

The work breakdown structure:
- Is derived from the project objectives and the project products, services, or results
- Provides a means for defining the total scope of work
- Ensures that work elements are defined and related to only one specific work effort so activities are not omitted or duplicated
- Is used as a framework for defining project tasks or activities.

The WBS is the key tool used to assist the project manager in defining the work to be performed to meet the objectives of a project. Developing the WBS is a four-step process that focuses on the products, services, or results to be delivered to the customer or end user. It provides a framework for organizing and decomposing the work to a suitable level of detail for planning and control. The concept was initially developed the Department of Defense and NASA in the early 1960s and has been a key component of project management ever since.

NOTES

1. M.L. Keene, *Effective Professional Writing* (Lexington, MA: D.C. Heath and Company, 1987), p. 32.
2. Project Management Institute Standards Committee, *A Guide to the Project Management Body of Knowledge (PMBOK® Guide)* (Upper Darby, PA: Project Management Institute, 2000).
3. *PMBOK® Guide*, p. 97.
4. *DoD and NASA Guide, PERT/Cost Systems Design* (Washington, D.C.: Office of the Secretary of Defense, National Aeronautics and Space Administration, June 1962), p. 3.
5. D.G. Malcolm, J.H. Roseboom, C.E.Clark, and W. Fazar, "Application of a Technique for Research and Development Program Evaluation," *Operations Research, The Journal of the Operations Research Society of America, 7*, No. 5 (September–October 1959): 646–669.
6. W. F. Munson, "A Controlled Experiment in PERTing Costs," Polaris Projection, GE Ordnance Department, November 1961.
7. *DoD and NASA Guide, PERT/Cost Systems Design* (Washington, D.C.: Office of the Secretary of Defense, National Aeronautics and Space Administration, June 1962).
8. *Ibid.*, pp. 26 –34.
9. National Aeronautics and Space Administration, *NASA PERT and Companion Cost System Handbook* (Washington, D.C.: Director of Management Reports, National Aeronautics and Space Administration, October 30, 1962).
10. Central PERT Department, Product Programming, Orlando Division, *PERT Time*, Martin Marietta, Document OR 3424, Volume I, September 1963, pp. 2-3.
11. U.S. Government Coordinating Group, *PERT Implementation Manual, Draft Copy*, August 1964.
12. Ibid., p. VI.4.
13. Department of Defense, MIL-STD-881, *Work Breakdown Structures for Defense Materiel Items* (Washington D.C.: Headquarters, Air Force Systems Command, Directorate of Cost Analysis, 1 November 1968).
14. DoD Regulation 5000.2-R.
15. Department of Defense, MIL-STD-881, Appendix E.
16. "PM Network®" is a trademark of the Project Management Institute, Inc., which is registered in the United States and other nations.
17. "*Project Management Journal®*" is a trademark of the Project Management Institute, Inc., which is registered in the United States and other nations.
18. PMI® Standards Committee, *PMI® Practice Standard for Work Breakdown Structures, Exposure Draft Version* (Newtown Square, PA: Project Management Institute, October 2000).
19. Project Management Institute Standards Committee, *A Guide to the Project Management Body of Knowledge (PMBOK® Guide)* (Upper Darby, PA: Project Management Institute, 2000), p. 58.
20. *PMBOK® Guide*, p. 58.
21. MIL-HDBK-881, paragraph 3.1.3.
22. Ibid., paragraph 2.2.5.
23. U.S. Government PERT Coordinating Group, p. VI.3.

CHAPTER 2

Work Breakdown Structure Fundamentals

The WBS represents a logical decomposition of the work to be performed and focuses on how the product, service, or result is naturally subdivided. It is an outline of *what* work is to be performed. Development of a WBS requires knowledge of how the output or deliverable components will be assembled or integrated to form the final product or knowledge of what the major areas of work are. This knowledge is required whether the final product is a report, an airplane, a building, an electronic system, a computer program, a wedding, a conference, a culture change, or any other output product from a project. It is necessary either to know something about the work that is to be done or to have access to subject matter expertise in order to involve the project team and other stakeholders in development of the WBS.

In this chapter, different algorithms for breaking down or subdividing project work are discussed. First, however, it is necessary to state an important rule that applies to all levels of all WBSs: the 100 percent rule.

THE 100 PERCENT RULE

The 100 percent rule is the most important criterion in developing a WBS and in evaluating the decomposition logic. It is as follows:

The next level decomposition of a WBS element (child level) must represent 100 percent of the work applicable to the next higher (parent) element.

In Figure 2-1, the 100 percent rule means that the combination of the work involved in landscaped grounds + garage + project management = 100 percent of the work to be performed in the garage project. There is no project activity that does not fit within one of these categories. In a top-down subdivision, most planners would follow this rule without prompting—at least to Level 2. Note, however, that the rule applies at all levels.

At the next level, the 100 percent rule means that the work in the garage element consists of work related to materials + foundation + walls + roof + utilities; there is no work on the garage itself that does not fit under one of

FIGURE 2-1   Garage Project

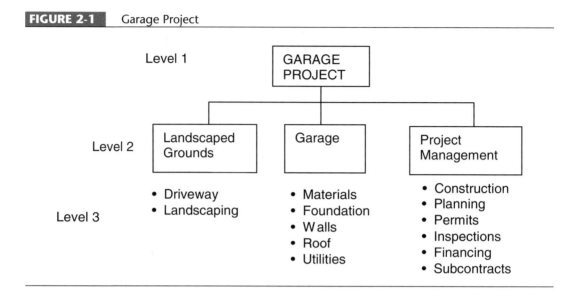

these elements. Looking back to Figure 1-4, the "walls" element is represented 100 percent by the walls and siding + windows + garage door + service door + assembly elements at Level 4. Again, these five elements encompass all the work on the walls. Note that the "assembly" element is necessary to account for the work of installing or integrating the work of the other independent elements.

Remember, the primary reason to have a WBS is to ensure that all the work packages and activities that must be accomplished for a successful project are identified. The 100 percent rule also applies at the activity level: The work represented by the activities in each work package must add up to 100 percent of the work necessary to complete the work package. In this manner, the project manager can be reasonably assured that all the work necessary for the project's successful completion has been planned and scheduled. This is an important rule because it helps the person developing the WBS to constantly question himself or herself on understanding the breadth and depth of the project's work.

It is recommended and common for the project team to collegially develop or at least review the WBS in detail. Subject matter experts will always look to make sure their specialty is included in the work, and they can contribute to ensure that the WBS is complete and as accurate as possible. For manufacturing projects, for example, it is useful to elicit input from manufacturing engineers or tooling engineers for the identification of probable subassemblies. In software projects, it is useful to elicit input from systems analysts, programmers, and database specialists. For our garage example, input from an experienced carpenter or garage-builder would be useful.

Not all WBSs are based on products (as discussed in Chapter 6). The rule still applies: The sum of the work in the child elements must equal 100 percent of the work represented by the parent element—even if the parent element is a general term like "system engineering" or "research." The use of bottom-up cost estimating—estimating the costs of every activity or work package and summing the data up the WBS hierarchy into a total project cost—is based on the critical assumption that the WBS is developed following the 100 percent rule.

One of the common ways to develop a WBS is from the bottom up; this is especially useful if the output product of the project is a service. All the project activities are listed first in a brainstorming session and then grouped into logical work packages or lower level WBS elements. These are, in turn, summarized into higher level elements. The 100 percent rule is followed at each level.

The following questions are asked at each level:

- Does the sum of the work represented by the child elements equal 100 percent of the effort summarized in each parent element?
- Is any work missing?

Experience has indicated that asking these questions invariably results in additional activities being added, and several iterations of the WBS structure may be performed until a sound WBS is developed.

The importance of the 100 percent rule cannot be overstated in the use of the WBS as a framework for planning. If the decomposition at each level follows the 100 percent rule down to the activities, then 100 percent of the relevant activities will have been identified when it is time to prepare the project schedule. And 100 percent of the costs or resource requirements will be identified in the planning phase.

ANATOMY OF A WBS

There are different types of projects and, therefore, different types of WBSs, each with unique elements. All WBSs have two or more of the five types of Level 2 elements as shown in Figure 2-2.

The first three types of elements are derived from the three types of projects, as indicated in the definition of a project in the *PMBOK® Guide*: "A temporary endeavor undertaken to create a unique *product, service, or result*."[1] For all types of projects there are one or more deliverables or outputs

FIGURE 2-2 Generic Work Breakdown Structure

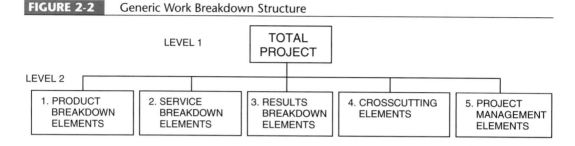

that are the basis for developing the WBS. The last two elements in Figure 2-2 are supporting elements necessary to completely define the scope of a project and meet the 100 percent rule.

These five types of elements are as follows:

1. **Product Breakdown**—The subdivision based on the physical structure of the product(s) being delivered is the most common basis for a WBS and the easiest WBS to develop. These projects have a tangible output product: software, a building, a dam, an airplane, a user's manual, etc.; all have a natural structure.

2. **Service Breakdown**—Service projects do not have a tangible, structured deliverable. The output is a defined body of work done for others: conference, party, wedding, vacation trip, etc. The work breakdown is a logical collection of related work areas.

3. **Results Breakdown**—Results projects do not have a tangible, structured deliverable. The output is the consequence of a process that results in a product or a conclusion: cancer research, new drug development, culture change, etc. The work breakdown is a series of accepted steps.

4. **Cross-Cutting Element**—This is a breakdown of items that cut across the product, such as architectural design, assembly, or system test. These usually are technical and supportive in nature. There may be more than one element of this characteristic at Level 2. While there is no restriction, these types of cross-cutting elements are rare in service or results projects.

5. **Project Management**—This is a breakdown of the managerial responsibilities and managerial activities of the project. It includes such items as reports, project reviews, and other activities of the project manager or his or her staff. (Conceptually, these are the overhead of the project.) Normally, there is only one of this type of WBS element, but it exists on *all* projects as a Level 2 element.

Product Projects Breakdown

The product breakdown is the decomposition of the natural physical structure of the output product being developed. This is apparent in Figure 1-1, the elephant breakdown structure. For building a garage, Level 2, the product would be garage, and Level 3, materials, foundation, walls, roof, utilities, and assembly, as illustrated in Figure 1-4. There may be more than one output product or major deliverable at Level 2. For the garage project, the landscaping and grounds is a secondary end item or deliverable; the project is not complete until all the plants have been planted and the ground prepared as described in the contract statement of work or drawing. An operator's manual may be an additional output or deliverable item if the project is a new high-speed lawn mower. If writing a book, the physical book would be the deliverable. If you were developing software, the documented source code, the manuals, and the CD-ROM with the executable program and installation software would be deliverables.

The product breakdown usually has more levels than the cross-cutting or project management sections. Some parts of the product breakdown may require decomposition to a greater level than others because of the nature of the product and its components. This can be seen in the WBS for the garage, Figure 1-4. If a major component of the garage, such as the foundation, is to be subcontracted, it becomes a work package and the lowest level necessary in the WBS. Further decomposition of the WBS would be the responsibility of the subcontractor, and the foundation could be considered a subproject. In large projects, such as construction of a new athletic stadium, subcontractor WBSs may have many levels. In product breakdowns, work packages can be assigned to either organizations or individuals, but specific resources are assigned only at the activity level.

Service Projects Breakdown

A WBS for a project where there is no tangible product, but where the objective is a *service* provided for a person or for a group, has a second type of WBS element and a different approach to decomposition. The decomposition is based on a logical grouping of similar and related work elements, functions, or skills. For example, all the work related to lodging on a project whose objective was a vacation trip to Asia could be located under the "lodging" element, which could be further decomposed to the city where the lodging was to occur. Activities may include making reservations, getting confirmation, making deposits, getting maps or directions, etc. There is usually a main event or objective for this type of project such as a wedding, a dinner party, or a conference. In these types of projects, all the WBS elements except project management represent a type of service provided or performed or arranged. This is illustrated in the WBS presented in Figure 2-3.

These types of WBSs are frequently developed initially from the bottom up, starting with a list of activities and grouping them into logical categories or functions. The basis for each Level 2 element is that it represents a logical grouping of tasks that can be discretely described. Further, each element at every level lends itself to being assigned to a single person or organization for performing or coordinating the group of work described in the element descriptor.

The decomposition of the Level 2 and lower elements is based on the criteria that the child elements are related to the parent, and the key word is *grouping*. For example, the breakdown of "transportation" could be 1. airport; 2. hotel-conference shuttle; 3. tour buses, etc.—all related to transportation. Also, note that the breakdown of "presentations" in Level 3 includes Level 4 elements that all relate to the presentations. This is different from a product WBS where the next level breakdown would be parts of the presentation and not just related items.

Adding elements at Level 2 also focuses attention on the function and can improve the planning. For example, in Figure 2-3, if security is a concern, it should be added at Level 2, rather than being spread at Level 3 or lower

FIGURE 2-3   Service WBS—International Conference Project

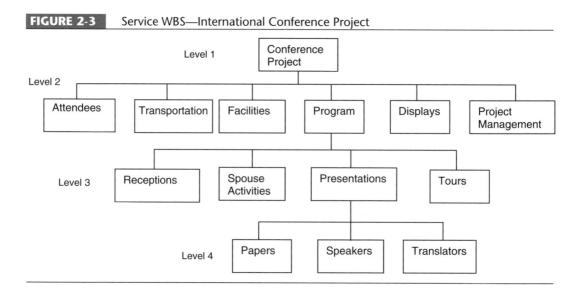

in other elements. In this manner, all aspects of security would be grouped and focused, and it is more likely that all important security tasks would be identified.

It is important to remember that the 100 percent rule applies, and the WBS needs to be analyzed for completeness at every level by the project team. Every task needs a WBS parent; in the process of brainstorming the task list, additional WBS elements may need to be added. Getting stakeholders involved in developing the WBS for a new class of project is more important in a service project than in a product or results project since there is no natural structure or sequence of elements to provide a hierarchy. However, if one worked for an events management firm, one would have a template or normal hierarchy based on previous projects.

Frequently, a large number of detailed activities need to be performed under each work package, like a checklist. The planning and scheduling document may be a combination of (1) a network to identify sequential relationships of major tasks, and (2) checklists to make sure that all the small details are identified and assigned. The WBS for a service project works well as a template for future similar projects. All big weddings are similar in the major functions: they need a church (or synagogue, mosque, etc.), attendants, receptions, showers, invitations, etc. Likewise, the WBSs for all conferences, parties, vacation trips, etc., are similar at least at Level 2 and perhaps at Level 3.

Results Projects Breakdown

Similar to a service project, the *results* type of project does not have a well-structured primary product as a deliverable but may have several products that collectively achieve the desired result. A results project has a series of planned, well-defined steps and is a process-based project.

Figure 2-4 is the WBS for a project whose result is the implementation of a Hazard Analysis Critical Control Point (HACCP) system in a food processing plant. This project's objective is to convert a traditional food processing line from one where quality is achieved by inspecting the end product to one where quality is planned-in through process controls applied at various critical control points.

In this type of project where the result is the successful implementation of an HACCP system, the same six steps are performed for each processing line or project. It is the same whether it is frozen seafood cakes, packaged chicken parts, or canned soup. There is also a series of steps at Level 3 and below that are prescribed and performed. Because every plant is different and

FIGURE 2-4   Results WBS—HACCP Implementation Project

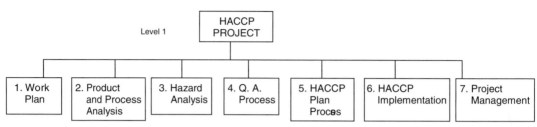

every project is unique, the intermediate outputs from each step are similar in name but quite different in content. Therefore, for similar results-type projects, the WBSs for the top levels are the same or very similar if the same result is to be achieved, i.e., an HACCP system for safe processed food.

In another example, the Level 2 and 3 elements (or steps) for a project to develop a new drug to be approved by the Food and Drug Administration are similarly required and controlled, as are many of the Level 3 elements. The acceptable or required process to be followed by each class of project establishes the elements at Level 2 and the Level 3 elements may also be prescribed. The decomposition is based on the process steps necessary to achieve the project objectives.

Again, the 100 percent rule applies and the team must carefully review the child elements of each parent at each level to ensure that all the work is identified. Persons familiar with or expert in the process should be used in this analysis. The goal is the same as with any WBS: to ensure that all the work is identified that must be performed to meet the project objectives.

Cross-Cutting Elements

The cross-cutting elements transect the peer WBS elements at each level and represent work that either supports the product category's development or content or is the next step in a process that results in a product. An example of the former is an element such as architectural design; an example of the latter would be final inspections of some products or system test in others. There may be more than one element of this characteristic at Level 2. In general, the more complex the project, the more likely there are multiple cross-cutting elements. As a rule, all projects have project management as one of the cross-cutting elements.

Cross-cutting elements often involve secondary or intermediate deliverables such as analytical reports that support the product deliverables. Where data deliverables exist that support the primary hardware (or software) product deliverable, they are frequently identified as a subdivision or work package under a cross-cutting element.

Analysis of many different WBSs identifies four types of cross-cutting elements:

1. Integrative
2. Analytical
3. Process
4. Project management.

The first three can occur at Level 2 or any lower level of the WBS, but project management is normally a Level 2 element.

An *integrative* element represents work that integrates two or more peer WBS elements. This is illustrated graphically in Figure 2-5 in the *assembly* element.

In the simplified example in Figure 2-5, the product breakdown of the bicycle includes the frame, seat, pedals and gears, and handlebars. The *assembly* work element is integrative since it represents the work involved in combining the other four elements. This *work* element is often missed when first developing a WBS or is implicitly assumed to be work that is part of the

FIGURE 2-5   Example of WBS with Integrative Element

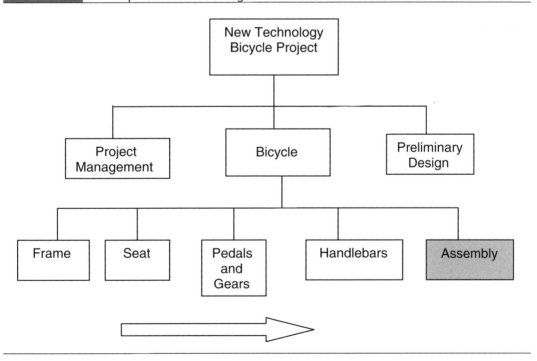

next higher or parent element. This assumption violates the 100 percent rule that states that the sum of the work of the elements at a child level is 100 percent of the parent. The work flows from the other WBS peer elements to the *integrative* element. It should be noted that Figure 1-4 also includes the integration WBS element of assembly at Level 4 under the Level 3 wall element.

An *analytical* element represents analytical activity that spans the work elements of a common parent. This is illustrated graphically in Figure 2-6 in the sample WBS for a project that included development of a personal computer.

In Figure 2-6, *system analyses* is a cross-cutting analytical element in the WBS. This element cuts across all the other elements at the same level and below in the WBS. The system analyses affect the development and content of the other WBS elements. Information flows from the analytical element to the other elements and impacts their design, development, or content. If the project were to write a book or prepare a report, a WBS element *research* at Level 2 would be an analytical-type element, with the information flowing from the research work performed to affect the contents of the other elements of the book.

FIGURE 2-6   Example of WBS with Analytical Element
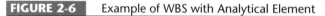

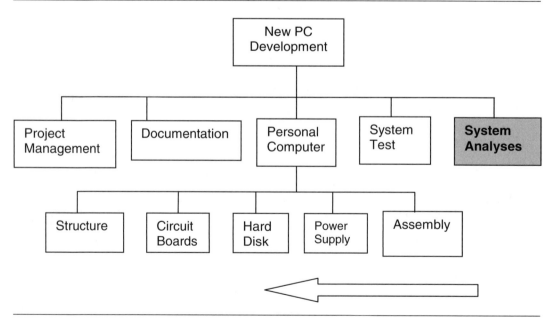

The next level of decomposition below an analytical element is often a set of work elements that are of a similar type as the parent, such as occurs in a parent element in a service project. For example, the next level below a *system engineering* element may be a group of similar engineering functions such as reliability engineering, maintainability engineering, and value engineering. The outputs of these functions are often data deliverables such as a reliability plan or a reliability analysis and are specified in the contract statement of work or a contract data requirements list.

Depending on the nature of the project, the Level 2 element may be even more general, such as simply *analyses,* and include such items as needs analysis, economic analysis, and demand analysis. This type of element is similar to the elements in a service project and represents a grouping of similar or related work that is necessary for the project.

A *process* element represents a next step in a work progression. It is similar to an *integrative* element but is more related to the flow of work than the grouping or combination of several elements. This is illustrated graphically in Figure 2-7.

The WBS element *test and evaluation* is cross-cutting and also the next step in a development process. At the level shown, the work performed in the *test and evaluation* element "cuts across" the other elements at the same level. It would require manuals, support equipment, the air vehicle (airplane), and maintenance facilities to do the testing work. The work flows into the direction of the process. Note that the other four Level 2 items are product deliverables.

FIGURE 2-7   Example of WBS with Process Element

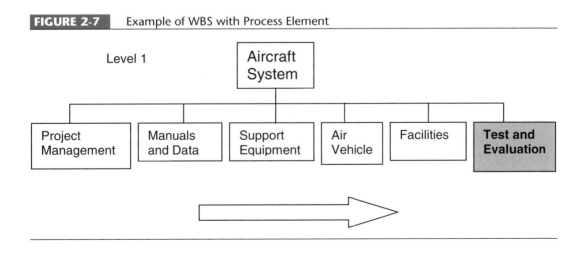

In Figure 2-8, *system test* is a process element since it is the next step in the process of preparing a personal computer for delivery to the customer. The work flows along the steps in the process. Also, the shaded work packages of the parent circuit boards are all process WBS elements leading to the intermediate deliverable of circuit boards.

Project Management

While all WBSs have one or more of the first four types of WBS elements, the elements do not always occur in every WBS. However, project management is a special category of cross-cutting element that occurs universally and has characteristics of the integrative, analytical, or process elements within it at lower levels. The reason is that all projects have project managers and they perform work in support of the project.

The 100 percent rule requires that the sum of the WBS elements at each level represent 100 percent of the work of the parent. Since the project

FIGURE 2-8   Example of WBS with Process Elements

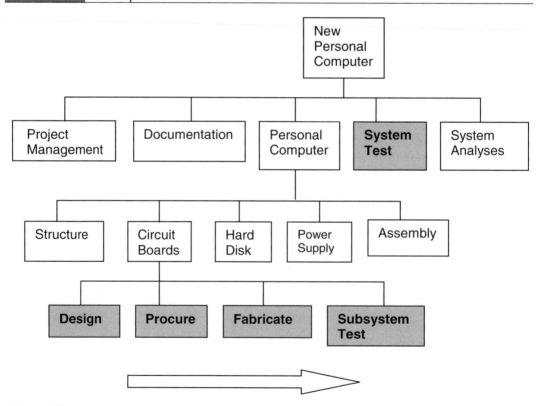

manager expends resources, work is involved and must be included. The labor cost and other expenses of the project manager and the project management office may or may not be charged to the project as a direct cost; however, resources are consumed and project management activities are performed.

Figure 2-9 contains a list of typical work packages and activities performed in project management. Level 4 in Figure 2-9 consists predominantly of work packages. The exceptions are the two zero duration activities, *contract award* and *complete project*, which are useful milestones in schedules. The advantages of their inclusion in this list and their usage are explained later in this chapter, in the section Numbering the WBS.

FIGURE 2-9   Project Management WBS Element Decomposition

PROJECT MANAGEMENT (Level 2)	
Level 3	Level 4 Work Packages
PROJECT START AND FINISH	Contract Award Complete Project
MEETINGS AND REVIEWS	Kick-off Meeting Monthly/Quarterly Project Reviews Corporate Reviews In-Process Review Close-out Meeting Action Item Tracking System
REPORTS	Monthly Progress Report Annual Report Budget/Financial Status Report
PLANS	Project Charter Master Schedule Project Plan (Current and Future Phases) Risk Management and Other Plans Project Financing and Budget
CONTROL	Schedule Tracking Cost Tracking Earned Value Management Analysis Variance Analysis Corrective Action Work-Arounds
ADMINISTRATIVE	Project Management Office Space/Relocation Correspondence Control System
PROJECT SUPPORT	Procurement/Purchasing Subcontract Management Contract Management

Frequently, some of the Level 4 items are routinely furnished by the parent organization and may not appear in the project WBS. In addition, some items may warrant their own Level 2 status if there is a significant amount of work performed and attention needs to be focused on it through the WBS. In any event, if work and resources are involved in any of the elements, those resources and the work should be reflected in the project plans. In addition, one of the rules of planning is to include the item if it is not automatically performed.

The 100 percent rule applies to all the work at Levels 3 and 4; all important work packages or activities must be included. The planning and resource allocations must address the large amount of work involved in managing a project.

WBS DICTIONARY

A WBS dictionary is a document that defines and describes the work to be performed in each WBS element. The information provided does not need to be lengthy, but it should sufficiently describe the work to be accomplished. Some organizations have found it useful to use a form to facilitate gathering WBS dictionary information. A typical form is presented in Figure 2-10.

The data on the form are all that are needed for the minimum dictionary. In some organizations, however, more data are gathered when applicable, such as budget, schedule, deliverables, and earned value management data that may be part of a specific WBS element. Such data are useful for work packages but may not be applicable for summary, higher level elements.

The following is a typical WBS dictionary description for a WBS element named *training* that might occur at Level 2:

WBS 1.4 Training. This element contains deliverable training services, manuals, accessories, and training aids and equipment used to facilitate instruction through which customer personnel will learn to operate and maintain the system with maximum efficiency. The element includes all effort associated with the design, development, and production of deliverable training equipment, and instructor and student guides as defined in the list of deliverables as well as the delivery of training services.

One advantage of a WBS dictionary is the discipline of describing the work in each element in words. Frequently, the brief, summary descriptions of WBS elements are vague or misunderstood and the dictionary can dispel any miscommunication that might result.

FIGURE 2-10   Sample WBS Dictionary Form

WBS DICTIONARY FORM
Project Name: _____   Date: _____
WBS Number: _____   WBS Name: _____
Parent WBS Number: _____   Parent WBS Name: _____
Responsible Individual/Organization (if applicable) _____
Description of Work:
Child WBS Number: _____   Child WBS Name: _____
Child WBS Number: _____   Child WBS Name: _____
Child WBS Number: _____   Child WBS Name: _____
Child WBS Number: _____   Child WBS Name: _____
Prepared by: _____Approved by: _____Date: _____
Title: _____   Title: _____

Some planners have found it useful to describe the WBS elements in terms of the activities performed in the element. This has the advantage of clarifying the work in the element without the need for a WBS dictionary. However, the use of activity nomenclature can be confusing and may tend to lose some of the discipline required for a noun-product based WBS. Another of the drawbacks of using activity-based WBS element descriptors is the difficulty of evaluating whether or not the 100 percent rule has been violated.

A WBS dictionary describing the work in each element can readily be converted into a comprehensive statement of work for a project or subproject and the author can be confident that it addresses all the work to be performed. The total project scope is thereby clearly and comprehensively defined.

WORK PACKAGES

The lowest level of the WBS is defined as the *work package level*, which provides a logical basis for defining activities or assigning responsibility to a specific person or organization. The primary purpose of the WBS is to make sure that all the work that is to be performed on the project is identified. A WBS is decomposed to the work package level; however, beyond the WBS, the work must be subdivided to the point where adequate planning and control can be accomplished. This is ultimately below the work package at the activity level where network planning is performed. Each activity has a specified and expected duration, resources, cost, performance, and output summarized into the work package. (This is discussed in more detail in the section, Use of the WBS to Develop Activities.) Each work package should have a single person or organization identified and responsible for the performance of the work.

A work package is the collection of activities performed by a specific organization, usually with a specific cost account number for a particular WBS element. This could be a large subcontracted package of work. A work authorization form or some equivalent document that specifies the budget level, start and completion dates, responsible organization, and brief statement of the work to be performed usually authorizes the work performed in a work package. Figure 2-11 illustrates the relationship between the WBS, work packages, and activities for Project X.

Cost control is often impractical at the activity level because of the difficulty of collecting actual cost data. However, cost control usually can be exercised at the work package level or higher where actual cost data can be accumulated. The *cost account* is the term used to describe the management control point at which actual cost can be accumulated and compared to budgeted costs for work performed." This is referred to as *earned value* BCWS in earned value management systems.[2]

APPROPRIATE LEVEL OF DETAIL

How much detail should be included in the WBS? There are many answers to this question. Generally, the part of the WBS that focuses on the product breaks down to a lower level than the cross-cutting elements. Raz and Globerson have developed a set of criteria to be used to determine

FIGURE 2-11   WBS, Work Package, and Activity Relationship

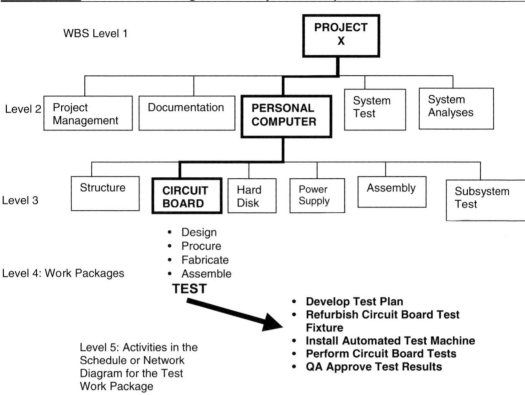

the extent of the decomposition of the WBS.[3] Their criteria, with some revisions, are illustrated in Figure 2-12.

In general, the work packages should be discrete, easily defined and managed, and the work content planned and scheduled by activities.

USE OF THE WBS TO DEVELOP ACTIVITIES

The specific mechanism used to develop activities and a set of criteria for defining activities are described in the following sections.

The WBS and Activities

After ensuring that the project's entire scope is addressed, the primary function of the WBS is to facilitate the identification and definition of the project's activities that need to be performed. In Chapter 1, the WBS was described as noun-based down through the work packages. Activities are verb-based because that is where the action is. This is also illustrated in Figure

FIGURE 2-12 Appropriate Level of Detail

Y/N	SHOULD THE WORK PACKAGE BE DECOMPOSED FURTHER?
	The greater the number of positive answers to the following questions, the stronger the justification for breaking down the work package
Y/N	**Question**
	Is there a need to improve the accuracy of the cost and duration estimates?
	Is more than one individual responsible for the work contents?
	Is there a need to know precisely the timing of activities internal to the work package?
	Is there a need to cost-out activities internal to the work package?
	Are there any dependencies between the internal activities and other work packages?
	Are there any significant time breaks in the execution of the work processes internal to the work elements?
	Do resource requirements within the work package change over time?
	Do the prerequisites differ among the internal deliverables within the work element?
	Are there any acceptance criteria applicable before completion of the entire work package?
	Can a portion of the work to be performed within the work package be scheduled as a unit?
	Are there any specific risks that require focused attention to a portion of the work package, requiring further division to separate them?
	Is the work package understood clearly and completely to the satisfaction of the various stakeholders?

Source: T. Raz and S. Globerson, "Effective Sizing and Content Definition of Work Packages," *Project Management Journal,* December 1998:17–23. Adapted with permission.

2-11. The WBS provides the outline structure for Gantt charts and network planning. In addition, it outlines what work will be performed; the activities describe the actions necessary to perform that work. This is illustrated in the hypothetical time-sharing system project (see Figure 2-13). Note that in this figure, the WBS elements are in bold and are in adjective/noun form; the activities are in italics in verb/adjective/noun form at the level below the WBS.

This example illustrates the relationship of the WBS to the schedule and to network planning. The individual activities are linked in the project management software into a precedence network and displayed in Gantt format on the screen and when normally printed out.

The manner in which the WBS is arrayed can make schedules easier to read and use. Put the project management element at the top of the WBS and numbered 1.0 as shown in Figure 2-13. If there is any natural process flow at Level 2 of the WBS, it should go from left to right in the graphic

---

FIGURE 2-13 Example of WBS Elements and Activities

Time Sharing System (TSS) Project

1.0 Project Management
    1.1 Project Start and Complete
        1.1.1 Go Ahead
        1.1.2 Complete Project
    1.2 Project Meetings
        1.2.1 Prepare for Kickoff Meeting
        1.2.2 Start Kickoff Meeting
    1.3 Project Reports
        1.3.1* *Prepare Interim Progress Report
        1.3.2 *Deliver Interim Progress Report*
2.0 TSS Requirements Specification
    2.1 Initial TSS Requirements Specification
        2.1.1 Create Initial TSS Requirements Specification
        2.1.2 Review Initial TSS Requirements Specification
        2.1.3 Update Initial TSS Requirements Specification
    2.2 Final TSS Requirements Specification
        2.2.1 Review Final TSS Requirements Specification
        2.2.2 Approve Final TSS Requirements Specification
3.0 TSS Design Specification
    3.1 **Initial TSS Design Specification**
        3.1.1 Create Initial TSS Design Specification
        3.1.2 Review Initial TSS Design Specification
        3.1.3 Update Initial TSS Design Specification
    3.2 Final TSS Design Specification
        3.2.1 Review Final TSS Design Specification
        3.2.2 Approve Final TSS Design Specification
4.0 TSS Software
    4.1 TSS Module 1
        4.1.1 Code TSS Module 1
        4.1.2 Unit Test TSS Module 1
    4.2 TSS Module 2
        4.2.1 Code TSS Module 2
        4.2.2 Unit Test TSS Module 2
    4.3 Integrate Modules
        4.3.1 System Test Integrated Modules
        4.3.2 Complete TSS Software

Source: Cindy Berg and Kim Colenso, "Work Breakdown Structure Practice Standard Project—WBS vs. Activities," *PM Network*, April 2000, p. 71. Adapted with permission.

version of the WBS or top to bottom in the outline version. The result is that the schedules will be displayed more naturally.

A useful device to assist in scheduling is establishing a special work package under project management for the start and complete events of the project. Included in the work package are the two zero duration activities that identify the start and completion.

In Figure 2-14, the data of Figure 2-13 have been entered into MS Project 98® to illustrate the use of the WBS as an outline for structuring the schedule. If the 100 percent rule is followed and the WBS is input into the project management software, it is an easy and swift task to identify all the project's activities and array them in a logical schedule format. The *activities* are the basic building blocks of the project. As has been stated previously, it should be noted that the goal of the WBS is to ensure that all these building blocks are identified.

Activity Definition

Experience has shown that defining activities or tasks is not as easy as it looks. Too often, there is inadequate definition and poor schedules, which result in communication problems. Activity definition is extremely important since activities are the building blocks for planning and controlling the project. Activities are defined in the *PMBOK® Guide* as an element of work performed during the course of a project.[4] An activity normally has an expected duration, an expected cost, and expected resource requirements, according to the *PMBOK® Guide's* definition. The definition should also state that a single person or organization responsible and accountable for work performed characterizes an activity.

Although infrequently specified explicitly at the detail level in project planning, activities also have performance requirements as well as specified outputs or results. If the activity is vague, it needs to be redefined.

A most important consideration is: *The activity may not be performed if it is not in the plan.* In fact, the reason to have a written plan is to ensure that the need for the activity is communicated to the appropriate stakeholders, including those persons responsible for predecessor and successor activities as well as the person responsible for performing the activity.

If some of the activities identified for the time sharing (TSS) project in Figures 2-13 and 2-14 are scrutinized, it is possible to see how the criteria are met. The TSS requirements specification and the TSS design specification are well-defined documents and the activities involved are all clear. The outputs are tangible—something is done to the document.

FIGURE 2-14   Time Sharing System (TSS) Project

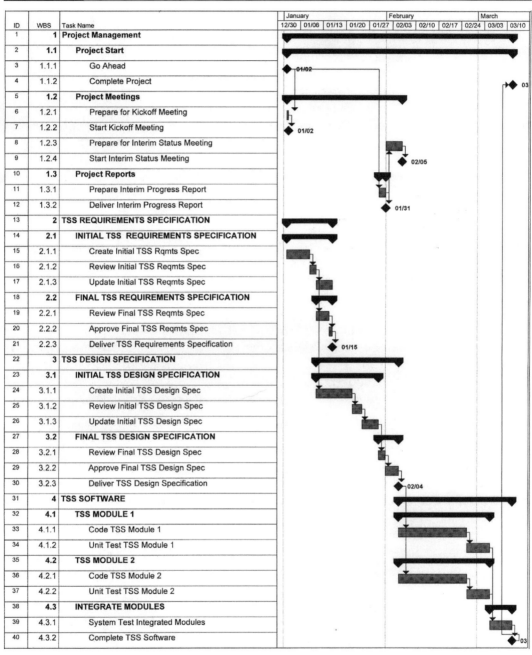

Characteristics of an Activity

- Work is performed and described in terms of a verb, adjective, and noun—there is action performed.
- A single person or organization is responsible for the work—more than one resource may be assigned to an activity, but one person is in charge of delivering the output. If this is not the case, the item needs further decomposition or joint responsibilities should be clarified.
- It has defined start and finish points—there is either a specific predecessor activity or event that must be completed first or a specific date on which the activity is scheduled to start; the scheduled end date is based on the estimated duration, baseline duration, or scheduled duration of the activity.
- Usually, there is a tangible output or product at completion—projects occasionally have level-of-effort activities or support activities without clearly defined outputs; however, the primary activities have defined and measurable outputs. The point at which an activity is completed is determined by the availability of an output product that is used as input by a successor activity.
- It fits logically under an existing WBS element—if it does not, the activity is not part of the project, the WBS needs modification, or the activity is ambiguous and needs redefinition.
- It is of a size and duration that is sufficient for control—activities that are too long do not provide sufficient time for corrective action if problems arise; activities that are too short make the control cost more expensive than a problem that may arise. Kerzner suggests that activities ideally be 80 hours and less than 2 to 4 weeks; however, this may not be possible on very large projects.[5]
- Actual schedule status data can be collected for the activity—for schedule control, the start and end points must be sufficiently defined so that the start and finish of the activity can be reported.
- Actual cost (person-hour) data can be collected for the activity or work package that contains the activity—for cost or resource control, actual cost data or the actual expenditure of resources can be collected; obviously, if tracking actual expenditures is not required, this principle can be ignored.
- The labor and costs necessary to perform the activity can be estimated—the resource requirements must be able to be determined in the planning phase.
- The output of the activity is known or can be identified—outputs are frequently pieces of paper or other tangible proof of the activity being completed.
- The activity represents a significant effort in support of project objectives—trivial or incidental activities need not be included.
- Zero duration activities are milestones or events and represent the start or completion of another activity or set of activities—they should be included at the start and finish of the project and included to identify completion of key activities or groups of activities.

The activities of coding the software are similarly clearly defined. The output would be completed software code, probably hard copy as well as digital format, depending on the normal practices of the organization. Unit test is usually defined with the completion of a document provided by the quality control organization or someone providing a similar independent function.

INPUTS VERSUS OUTPUTS—RESOURCES VERSUS DELIVERABLES

It is important to understand the differences between the inputs to the project and the output products. The concept of an output or deliverable-oriented structure can be difficult to grasp.

Input versus Output Elements

For years, planning has been performed in terms of the organizations and resources doing the work, i.e., the inputs. The use of a WBS requires a different perspective—a focus on the output. The output is what is going to be produced: the product, service, or result. Project inputs include the labor and cost resources necessary to perform the work. They are essential, of course, but approaching project planning from this perspective risks missing major elements of work. Typical project inputs include cost elements such as those shown in Figure 2-15.

These items are not ignored in project planning; the assignment of inputs to individual activities is performed. Most current project management software programs have resource tables that contain lists and costs of project inputs. These items are selected from the resource table and assigned to individual activities for cost estimating and resource planning. In addition, pricing proposals are often required to be structured by categories similar to these and to include overhead rates. However, the primary purpose of the WBS concept is to develop a framework for planning that ensures that all the *work* is identified. Once this is accomplished, the assignment of resources and cost elements can be accomplished at the work package or activity level. The work can then be scheduled and sorted by input or organization as necessary to communicate requirements for work performance.

Deliverables versus Intermediate Outputs

Project deliverables, as defined previously, include any measurable, tangible, verifiable outcome of a project. They can be a product, service, or a result. There may be hundreds of deliverables on a large project, such as

FIGURE 2-15   Typical Project Inputs

- Computers
- Construction labor (electricians, carpenters, painters, roofers, etc.)
- Data processing support
- Engineering labor (draftsmen, mechanical engineers, structural engineers, reliability engineers, hydraulic engineers, software engineers, test engineers, etc.)
- Facility rental
- Graphic artists
- Individual resource names
- Manufacturing labor (machinists, assemblers, welders, mechanics, maintenance, etc.)
- Office supplies
- Organization names
- Production control labor
- Programming labor
- Purchased parts
- Quality control
- Raw material
- Secretarial support
- Supervision
- Telephone and fax
- Tooling engineering labor
- Travel
- Utility expense
- Writers

the ship system depicted in Figure 1-9, especially where many data items are required to support the product. Each one of these, as well as the related work, needs to be identified and included in the WBS. Deliverables need not only represent the product handed to the customer at the end of the project. Usually, intermediate outputs must be developed. Some examples may clarify further what is meant by the intermediate deliverable or intermediate output.

For the sample project of building a garage, the obvious output or deliverable is a completed garage. The WBS for the garage is shown in Figure 2-16 in outline format. The Level 2 elements, the first level of decomposition, are shown in bold. There are many intermediate outputs. One category of output includes the items that the project management office must produce to support the project. This includes intermediate outputs such as securing financing, developing and preparing subcontracts, and developing construc-

FIGURE 2-16   Garage Outputs

GARAGE WORK BREAKDOWN STRUCTURE—OUTLINE FORMAT
1   PROJECT MANAGEMENT
1.1   CONSTRUCTION PLANNING
1.2   PERMITS
1.3   INSPECTIONS
1.4   FINANCING
1.5   SUBCONTRACTS
2   GARAGE
2.1   MATERIALS
2.2   FOUNDATION
2.3   WALLS
2.4   ROOF
2.5   UTILITIES
2.5.1   ELECTRICAL
2.5.2   PLUMBING
3   LANDSCAPED GROUNDS
3.1   DRIVEWAY
3.2   LANDSCAPING

tion plans. A completed piece of paper shows when each activity is finished. Another category of intermediate outputs is the county permits that must be acquired; each inspection results in a certificate from the inspector or a signed inspection sheet. Actually, all the Level 2 items under project management represent work packages with intermediate outputs.

A sample of the first two levels of another WBS is illustrated in Figure 2-17 for a book project. Four Level 2 outputs are identified. One is project management, which includes the intermediate outputs of meetings, reports, and reviews. A second category—a cross-cutting analytical category—is the research necessary for writing various chapters. The third category—writ-

FIGURE 2-17   Book Project—Level 2 WBS

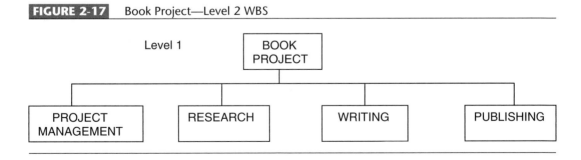

ing—includes the book contents. Research is not an input resource, but a category of intermediate work output delivered to the writing work area. The output of the writing element is not a completed book, but a set of completed chapters and items such as the table of contents and the cover. The fourth output—publishing—includes the reviews of completed drafts of the book and the actual printing of proofs and the final copies. (See Chapter 5 for the complete book project WBS.)

Neither of these WBSs includes labor or cost elements. As mentioned previously, they are identified with the activities and are input items identified at the work package or activity level.

NUMBERING THE WBS

In developing a WBS, coding or numbering the various elements and levels significantly improves the functionality of the WBS in various related applications. The coding can be done by any method, but it is important that it be consistent. Most organizations have standard codes. These codes can be used and modified to contain numeric/alpha elements that give a unique identification to each work activity. The resulting identification provides a label for scheduling, budgeting, tracking, replanning, assigning, and in general, communicating across the project. Many of the project management software packages allow one to enter the WBS codes and to use these codes for sorting data and preparing specialized reports.

There are many possible numbering systems for the elements of the WBS. The purpose of all numbering systems is to identify the WBS work element readily and where it fits in the overall project hierarchy. WBS elements frequently have similar names and the numbering system clearly identifies each discrete element.

A decimal numbering system as illustrated in Figure 2-18 is commonly used.

The decimal numbering system is precise and thorough, and can continue to whatever level is necessary. The system is illustrated in Figure 2-19 for the garage project. If there are several projects in an organization, and similar WBS elements in each, a prefix such as GP1 (garage project #1) could be added to discriminate between projects.

This numbering would be extended into all the activities in the schedule or network diagram so that every activity is discretely identified. This decimal outline numbering matches typical accounting systems numbering, which facilitates cost accounting, cost roll-up, and earned value systems.

FIGURE 2-18 Generic Decimal Outline Numbering

```
DECIMAL OUTLINE NUMBERING
1. [First major category]
       1.1. [Subheading]
       1.2. [Subheading]
2. [Second major category]
       2.1. [Subheading]
              2.1.1. [Detail]
              2.1.2. [Detail]
                     2.1.2.1. [Breakdown]
                     2.1.2.2. [Breakdown]
       2.2. [Subheading]
3. [Third major category]
```

Other internal systems using the WBS as an organizing framework are:
- Action item tracking—relating action items from meetings and reviews to WBS numbers
- Bills of material—the WBS number may be included in the part number or vice versa
- Change management—change proposals include WBS numbers
- Correspondence control—in addition to day files and organization files

FIGURE 2-19 Garage Project Numbering

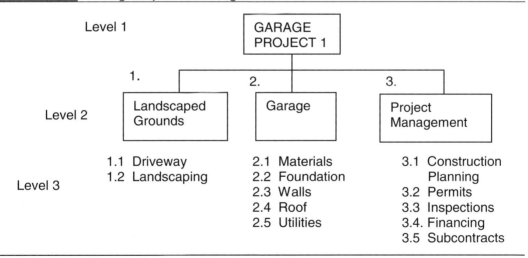

- Data management
- Drawing numbers—part of the drawing number includes the WBS number from the product WBS elements
- Report numbering
- Risk management—relating specific risks from the risk identification process to the WBS elements
- Subcontract numbering.

ALTERNATE STRUCTURE CONCEPTS

The concept of a WBS as an outline has been emphasized throughout this book. An outline is both an organized description of the project work and a plan for the work to be accomplished. In developing the outline, work may be identified that was not initially contemplated, and work may be eliminated that is not part of the project. The final WBS may go through several stages as the project becomes defined. A normal WBS contains very brief descriptions of the work elements—like a sketchy topical outline. This requires that the work be defined during the WBS development process; the final products may include a statement of work structured around the WBS or a WBS dictionary. However, in some cases, it may be preferable to identify the work elements with phrases or sentences.

The kind of outline—that is, WBS—you use should be determined by the project work structure itself, the culture of your organization, and your own thought processes. For most people, there is an interaction between defining work elements, thinking, and organizing. As one proceeds in the development of a WBS, it will probably be revised more than once, the order of work elements rearranged, work added, and work deleted.

The preferred approach to the development of the WBS is to make it a team effort. The team members will become intimately involved in the project and the definition of the work to be performed. This also helps ensure that all the work is identified since specialists and experts will make sure that the WBS covers their specialty areas.

When developing a WBS with a team, there are only two primary rules:
1. The 100 percent rule
2. Project management should be a Level 2 WBS element.

All the other rules, such as those listed in Chapter 6, can be tailored to fit the culture and used as guidelines.

There are differing opinions as to the best structure for a WBS. Translating Walker's concept of the outline structure for writing into a WBS structure, she says that the best organizing principles are inherent in the project itself and in the way the project is to be implemented.[6] For example, a project that is to be implemented in several different cities is best organized by structuring the work geographically at Level 2 and one of the other types of structures at Level 3.

A project where one organization will complete all its work and then pass it on to another for the next step is best organized by process steps at Level 2. A project that involves the tightly integrated design, development, and fabrication of a prototype is best organized by the structure of the deliverable product. Using the personal computer example, the principal alternate WBS constructs are illustrated in Figures 2-20 and 2-21.

Both of these WBSs should result in the same work packages and activities being defined, although the product WBS is more focused on deliverables. The two WBSs present different perspectives of the work content. The choice will depend on the culture and structure of the organization, the managerial style of the project manager, and other factors. If the 100 percent rule is followed, the end result should be the same.

The WBS in Figure 2-21, although it has a process flow, is not a results-type project. It is a project with a product focus that is structured with processes.

It is necessary to keep an open mind about how to structure a WBS and allow the project itself to suggest its own organization.

The *PMBOK® Guide* describes other kinds of breakdown structures to present project information.[7] These and others are as follows:

- **Organizational Breakdown Structure (OBS)** is a structure that is used to show which work components have been assigned to which organizational units. Preparing an OBS can be very confusing if the intent is to use it to define the work since it is organization- or input-oriented. The focus in developing a WBS must be on the work, not on organizations of people. One of the difficulties in developing a WBS is to move away from the paradigm of structuring work by organization function and instead to focus on the deliverable or output product. It is useful to develop the OBS after the project activities are all defined to provide a report or schedule of all the activities that are the responsibility of a specific organization, such as engineering design. Most project management software systems make it easy to add an organization or responsibility code to identify the organization. In some software packages, these fields are identified as OBS fields. Rad categorizes the OBS as "the most readily available structure."[8] He cautions that since companies frequently go through large organizational

FIGURE 2-20 Product-Based WBS

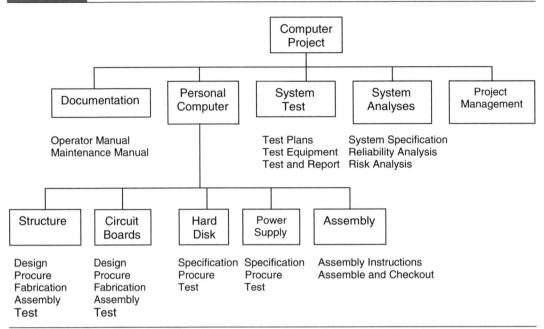

FIGURE 2-21 Process-Based WBS

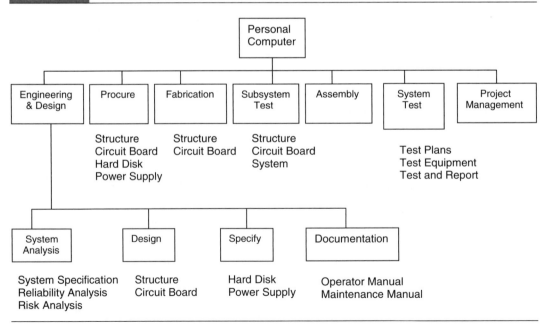

changes, "care must be taken to use the most recent data and to make updates as changes continue to occur within the organization."

- **Resource Breakdown Structure (RBS)** is described as a variation of the OBS and is typically used when work components are assigned to individuals. Rad has a somewhat different perspective of the RBS than that in the *PMBOK® Guide.*[9] He perceives the RBS as a logical and useful classification of the resources needed to accomplish a project's objectives. He also recommends developing a resource pool that is essentially a catalog of all the resources available to a project. To accomplish cross-project resource planning, the coding or categorization scheme of the resources in the pool needs to be the same for each project.

- **Bill of Materials (BOM)** presents a hierarchical view of the physical assemblies, subassemblies, and components needed to fabricate a manufactured product according to the *PMBOK® Guide.* However, a BOM, if available for a deliverable of a project, is useful for structuring the product section of the WBS. In fact, a summary or top-level BOM is essential for developing a WBS for most tangible products. A BOM by itself is not a WBS.

- The *PMBOK® Guide* also makes reference to a project breakdown structure (PBS). PBS is the term used in the 1960s and eventually dropped in favor of the WBS terminology. Archibald describes the PBS as identical to the WBS in his 1976 book.[10]

OTHER CATEGORIZATIONS

There is no one best categorization or subdivision of the project. It is sometimes desirable to use a different structure because of the situation or culture of the stakeholders. Various commonly used categorization schemes at the top levels follow:

- **Components of the product or service to be delivered:** Automobile—fenders, engine, hood, seats, frame, gas tank, etc.
- **Subsystems:** Airplane—hydraulic, electronics, structure, pneumatics, power plant, etc.
- **Projects:** Program—Project A, project B, project C, etc.
- **Process Phases:** Software—Requirements, design, coding, test, etc.
- **Time Phases:** Lifecycle—Conceptual, planning, implementation, etc.
- **Geographic Areas:** New York City—Brooklyn, Queens, Manhattan, etc.
- **Organizational Units (Phases):** Engineering, construction, etc.

On the surface, it appears that some of these categorizations are inputs, such as organizational units; however, that is really not the case. The items represent phases of the project discussed later. The WBS under each of the categories is still output- or deliverable-oriented. It is important that there is a logical framework for planning that is internally consistent and represents all the work to be performed on the project. The WBS is output-oriented.

Other categorizations are sometimes proposed:

- **Organization:** Engineering—Mechanical design, structural design, system analysis, etc.
- **Persons:** Small project—John, Mary, Ozzie, David, etc.
- **Cost Accounts:** Labor, travel, office supplies, etc.

These three categorizations are all input-oriented and therefore are not appropriate for a WBS. Organization names and codes, cost accounts, persons, and other inputs are appropriate for coding work packages and activities to provide reports or information sorted by these types of categories.

On occasion, persons attempt to link WBS elements or to use the WBS to assist in the sequencing of work. No matter whether the WBS has a process, systems, or product structure focus, the sequence of work is not the objective. The important aspect is whether the work required to deliver the project end items and meet the project objectives has been identified in enough detail to identify activities and resources and to assign responsibility.

On the surface, the work breakdown structure decomposition appears to be simple and straightforward. However, several different approaches can be taken, depending on the type of project and the category of work.

One rule that applies to all the methods is that the next level of decomposition of a WBS element must represent 100 percent of the work applicable to the next higher element. This is referred to as the "100 precent rule." When followed, it ensures that the WBS encompasses all the work on the project.

There are three types of project, based on the type of output: product, service, or result. The WBS for each type has it own characteristics and rules for decomposition. The "product" breakdown is a decomposition based on the natural physical structure of the output product being produced. The "service" breakdown is based on a logical grouping of similar and related work elements, functions, or skills. The "results" project has a series of planned and well-defined steps and is process-based.

In addition, there is another category for the WBS elements, referred to as "cross-cutting." Cross-cutting elements are usually technical and supportive in nature. The four basic types are: integrative, analytical, process, and "project management." The latter exists in all projects as a Level 2 element. Conceptually, the project management element represents the "overhead" of a project.

NOTES

1. Project Management Institute Standards Committee, *A Guide to the Project Management Body of Knowledge (PMBOK® Guide)* (Upper Darby, PA: Project Management Institute, 2000), p. 204.
2. Q.W. Fleming, *Put Earned Value (C/SCSC) into Your Management Control System* (Worthington, OH: Publishing Horizons, Inc., 1983), p.52.
3. T. Raz and S.Globerson, "Effective Sizing and Content Definition of Work Packages," *Project Management Journal*, December 1998: 17–23.
4. Project Management Institute Standards Committee, *A Guide to the Project Management Body of Knowledge* (Upper Darby, PA: Project Management Institute, 2000), p.197.
5. H. Kerzner, *Project Management: A Systems Approach to Planning, Scheduling and Controlling, 7th Ed.* (New York: John Wiley & Sons, 2001), p. 576.
6. M. Walker, *Writing Research Papers* (New York: W.W. Norton & Company, 1984), p. 90.
7. *PMBOK® Guide*, p. 61.
8. P. F. Rad, "Advocating a Deliverable-Oriented Work Breakdown Structure," *Cost Engineering 12* (December 1999).
9. Ibid., p. 35.
10. R.D.Archibald, *Managing High-Technology Programs and Projects* (New York: John Wiley & Sons, 1976), p. 141.

CHAPTER 3

Lifecycle Planning: Programs and Phases

All projects have phases and a project lifecycle. As the projects get larger in terms of resources and longer in duration, these phases become more pronounced. Various industries have special language or jargon to describe the various phases of larger projects. Large projects often become programs over time, and many projects are thought of or planned as programs from the start. In this chapter, the concept of a *program WBS* is introduced and related to the project WBS.

LIFECYCLE PHASES

The *PMBOK® Guide* presents a sample generic lifecycle of a project as illustrated in Figure 3-1.

One popular construct for defining the phases is as follows:

I. **Feasibility, Conceptual, or Initiation Phase**—conduct feasibility analyses and economic analyses; establish preliminary project objectives; prepare a preliminary WBS, a preliminary statement of work, and a project charter.

II. **Planning Phase**—firm up objectives and scope statement; define the work; develop the WBS; schedule the work, resources, and budget; and prepare the project plan.

III. **Execution or Implementation Phase**—perform the work; develop the products, services, or results.

IV. **Close-out Phase**—obtain final acceptance of deliverables; complete all financial, administrative, contractual, and personnel activities (project ends).

V. **Operations and Maintenance Phase**—the customer or sponsor uses the output of the project.

When the projects are small ones or have been contracted-out, many project managers are not involved in the first phase. A project may be assigned based on work or decisions made at higher levels in the organization or on the judgment of a senior manager. The organization may be serving as a

FIGURE 3-1   Sample Generic Lifecycle

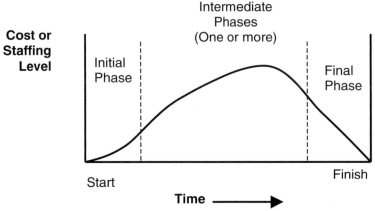

Source: *PMBOK® Guide*, p. 13. Reprinted with permission.

contractor or subcontractor, and the customer may perform the feasibility and possibly the planning phase and then the contract is awarded after a competitive procurement process.

Small projects frequently have an informal initial phase, especially office projects where a project may be the result of a meeting. For these, lifecycle considerations are not as important as for larger projects; however, the project manager must be aware of where the project is in the generic spectrum. Figure 3-2 is an abbreviated illustration of the lifecycle phases used by the Department of Defense for the acquisition of major products.

The description of these phases as included in the *PMBOK® Guide*[1] is as follows:

- **Concept and technology development**—paper studies of alternative concepts for meeting a mission need; development of subsystems/components and concept/technology demonstration of new system concepts. It ends with selection of system architecture and a mature technology to be used.

- **System development and demonstration**—system integration; risk reduction; demonstration of engineering development models; development and early operational test and evaluation. It ends with system demonstration in an operational environment.

- **Production and deployment**—low rate initial production (LRIP); complete development of manufacturing capability; phase overlaps with ongoing operations and support.

FIGURE 3-2   Sample Generic Lifecycle

Representative Lifecycle for Defense Acquisition			
Concept and Technology Development	System Development and Demonstration	**Production and Deployment**	Support
Pre-Systems Acquisition	Systems Acquisition (Engineering, Development, Demonstration, LRIP, and Production)		Sustainment and Maintenance

- **Support**—this phase is part of the product (not project) lifecycle and represents program-type ongoing activity. Projects may be conducted during this phase to improve capability, correct defects, upgrade the technology, etc.

A second example of lifecycle phases for a typical construction project is presented in Figure 3-3. At the end of the feasibility stage, the project "GO" decision is made. The end of the planning and design stage is defined by the letting of all major contracts. At the end of the construction stage, the installation is substantially complete, and at the end of the turnover and startup stage, the facility has been accepted and is in full operation.

If an operations and maintenance or a support phase is added as was done in the DoD example, then the project evolves into a program. Remember, the definition of a program is: *A group of related projects managed in a coordinated way. Programs usually include an element of ongoing work.*

A third and final example is illustrated in Figure 3-4. It is a description of the phases used by a museum for the development of a new exhibit. Because of the existence of the operation and maintenance phase of ongoing work, it will be referred to as a program.

Other industries have different lifecycle structures. While all these figures have several things in common, the important feature is that all the phases have well-defined outputs that must be completed before proceeding into the next phase. In effect, each phase is a project by itself: *a temporary endeavor undertaken to create a unique product, service, or result.* For each of the examples, each of the individual phases or stages meets the definition of a project.

FIGURE 3-3   Representative Construction Project Lifecycle

STAGE I FEASIBILITY	STAGE II PLANNING AND DESIGN	STAGE III CONSTRUCTION	STAGE IV TURNOVER AND STARTUP
• Project Formulation • Feasibility Studies • Strategy Design and Approval	• Base Design • Cost and Schedule • Contract Terms and Conditions • Detailed Planning • Solicitation	• Manufacturing and Material • Delivery • Civil Works • Installation • Testing	• Final Testing • Maintenance

LIFECYCLE WBS CONCEPTS

A specific WBS should be developed for the various phases of the lifecycle of a project. The basis for the discussion is the museum exhibit example outlined in Figure 3-4. The Museum Exhibit Program phase outputs are summarized in Figure 3-5. The lifecycle phases for the generic museum exhibit program are illustrated in Figure 3-6. They are referred to as projects.

The program WBS follows the rules outlined in Chapter 2 in the section entitled Anatomy, with only program management as a cross-cutting element. Each element has its own set of deliverables. Each of the elements is a project

FIGURE 3-4   Representative Museum Exhibit Lifecycle

Pre-Project (Blue Sky)	A. Project Definition	B. Planning	C. Development and Production	D. Closeout	E. Operation and Maintenance
Situation description, ideas and strategies	Concept development, research, evaluation, statement of purpose, project management, and planning	Space plans, exhibit plan, design package, script package, project managemen t, and planning	Complete designs, complete scripts, space prepared, exhibit fabrication and installation, project management , and planning	Evaluations, punch lists, training, administrative closeout, project management, and planning	Operation and maintenance, upgrades and revisions, project management

FIGURE 3-5 Outputs of Lifecycle Phases

MUSEUM EXHIBIT PROGRAM PHASE OUTPUTS

1. A document called an "Idea Statement" must be submitted and approved by a specified Committee before a project is established. Anyone can submit an Idea Statement and the contents of the Idea Statement are defined.

2. At the end of the Project Definition phase, a rather comprehensive document called a "Statement of Purpose Report" must be completed and approved. This document essentially describes what the exhibit is to do and for whom. A preliminary project team is formed, and tasks such as audience surveys, consulting with community groups, scholars, and other museum staff are performed. This document may have several iterations and must be approved by a number of persons from different organizations that make up an "Approval Team."

3. The Planning phase starts when the Statement of Purpose is approved and ends with an approved Project Plan and baselined schedules and budgets. In addition there is completion of 35% of the design and 60% of the script. In addition 50% of the visual materials, objects, and graphics are defined. Criteria exist for defining the percentages shown.

4. The Development and Production phase is actually subdivided into several sub-phases and many internal approvals are required. In addition, the end of this phase is defined by the Opening of the Exhibit.

5. The Closeout phase is defined as complete when all the work necessary to bring administrative closure is complete and the exhibit is turned over to the organization that will operate and maintain the exhibit until it closes.

6. The Operations and Maintenance phase continues until the exhibit is closed.

except for the ongoing operation and maintenance element, which contains a combination of processes and projects. The program level is defined as Level 0 so that the top level element of each project remains Level 1.

There are three types of project management WBS elements in a program organized and managed by lifecycle phases:

1. The traditional project management activities at Level 1 (relabeled program management) apply to activities that are overhead to the entire program and crosscut all phases.

FIGURE 3-6   Project WBS

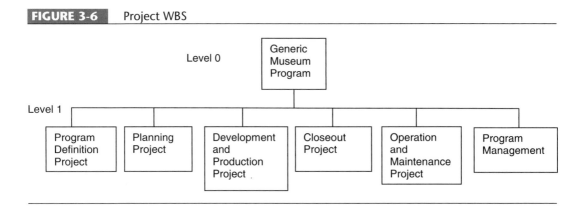

2. Project management activities that relate to the management of each phase as an independent Level 2 project.

3. Project management activities performed in one phase but that relate to subsequent phases; these are unique to lifecycle subprojects within a larger program framework.

The first category, program management, may not always exist. A project may evolve into a program and all project management elements are at Level 2. The existence of a program management level also implies that some effort is performed prior to the project definition phase. The outcome of the project definition phase may be the establishment of a program management function that provides program management support and performs project management functions for all phases.

The second category is the normal project management element of the WBS as described in Chapter 2.

The third category is somewhat different since it includes specific deliverables within the project management element that relate to later phases of the program. It is no longer just an overhead type of element but includes cross-cutting analytical elements as discussed in the Chapter 2 in the section entitled Anatomy. In each phase of the museum example in Figure 3-4, there are analytical WBS elements that relate to the planning of the subsequent phase and require input from the other work in the phase. For example, outputs of the project management element in the project definition phase are the WBS and scope statement for the planning phase and the preliminary WBS, schedule, and resource plans for the later phases.

Similarly, the project management element for the planning phase would include those elements that relate to management of the planning phase. It would also include the important output of the planning activity that results in a project plan for the subsequent development and production phase of the project, where most of the money and resources will ultimately be spent.

This is illustrated graphically in Figure 3-7 in the partial WBS. The complete project is presented at Level 2 with six elements labeled A through F. These six meet the 100 percent rule. Five of these, A through E, are also identified as projects and are phases of the program as well. A project phase is defined as: *A collection of logically related project activities, usually culminating in the completion of a major deliverable.*[2] As we have seen, each of these projects and/or phases meets this definition as well.

The program management element at Level 1 is neither a subproject nor a phase; it is a normal project management element. A possible decomposi-

FIGURE 3-7 WBS for Project Management in the Lifecycle

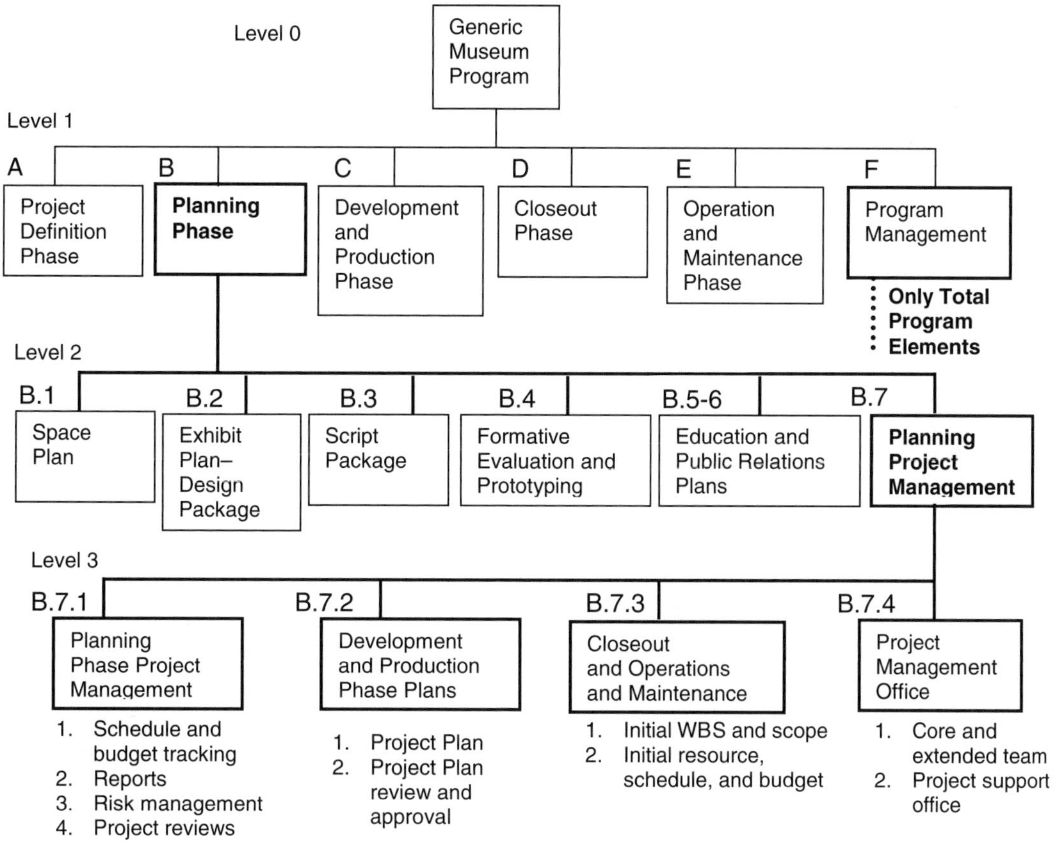

tion of this element, as shown in Figure 3-8, includes only total *program* elements.

This is not the only possible decomposition; various organizations may approach the structuring of the WBS program management element differently. For example, all the planning for the various phases can be included in the program management element rather than a part of each project management element within each phase. The important factor is to identify all of the work.

The decomposition of the planning phase/subproject (B) is shown in Figure 3-7. Elements B.1 through B.6 are normal Level 2 WBS elements and B.7 is a normal project management element except that it includes one of the major deliverables from this phase. The decomposition of planning project management has four major elements at Level 3: B.7.1 through B.7.4. The Level 4 decomposition of these elements is also shown in Figure 3-7 as numbered items under the Level 3 element.

The level 3 WBS elements consist of the following types of elements:

B.7.1 Planning phase project management—the normal, analytical project management effort that includes the work of managing the planning phase of the project.

B.7.2 Development and production phase plan—an integrative element; produces one of the major deliverables or outputs from this phase of the overall program. This element could have been arrayed at Level 2 but is normally considered work performed as part of the project management category. In this case, the plan is a cross-cutting element of both Level 2 and Level 3.

| FIGURE 3-8 | Program Management Decomposition |

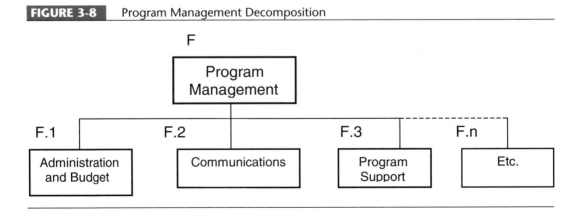

B.7.3 Closeout and operation and management phase plan—also an analytic element that produces a preliminary deliverable during this planning subproject phase. This deliverable will be completed prior to the end of the development and production phase.

B.7.4 Project management office—another normal WBS element under B.7 Planning Project Management and, in this case, represents the work performed by personnel resources supporting the project as part of the project management office.

These descriptions illustrate the differences in a WBS for a single project and for a set of projects or subprojects that make up the program lifecycle. The difference is the role of project management in integrating the project at several levels. Although the phases are different in terms of the work performed in each phase, they are all part of one larger program that is planned in its totality by the program manager and the project management office.

DEPARTMENT OF DEFENSE PROGRAM WBS AND THE LIFECYCLE

The Department of Defense (DoD) was a pioneer in lifecycle planning. Figure 3-2 illustrates the lifecycle for systems acquisition. The DoD concept of a program WBS is different from the multiphase project WBS previously described. The DoD program WBS focuses on the acquisition phases and the evolution of the program WBS as the system engineering and definition work progresses. It should be noted that the DoD definition of a program is closer to a superproject than the definition of a program in the *PMBOK® Guide*, because it only encompasses the acquisition phases and does not include the other lifecycle phases. The intent of the DoD program WBS is to provide the framework to plan and manage the acquisition of major DoD systems within the procedures and discipline prescribed by DoD. For this reason, DoD and the MIL-HDBK-881[3] have a narrower focus than the *PMBOK® Guide*.

From the DoD perspective, in order to use the WBS as a framework for the technical objectives of a program (in addition to its use as a management tool for cost and schedule control), the WBS *must* be product-oriented. The elements must represent identifiable work products, whether they are equipment, data, or related service products. The DoD approach ensures complete definition of the program effort to encompass the work performed by all participants, including prime contractors, contractors, and subcontractors.

The DoD *Handbook* does not preclude the use of the WBS to provide a service or result as discussed in this book; however, certain philosophies and terminology should be followed when major military hardware and software systems are being acquired.

PHASES WITHIN PROJECTS

Some organizations operate with a standard set of process steps as they proceed through a particular phase of a typical project. These are sometimes incorrectly referred to as lifecycle steps and include such items as *design—procure—fabricate—test* for a hardware product. For a software product, the steps may be *requirements—design—code—test.*

Because of the familiarity with this process within a particular organization, it is a temptation to structure the WBS accordingly even though the output is a product and not a result. It should be remembered that result projects have process elements at Level 2. It is important to keep the WBS focused on the output products and deliverables—and the decomposition should start there. There is no problem to structure a *program* WBS by lifecycle phases as discussed earlier in this chapter. That is a different issue.

Figure 3-9 presents an example of a partial program WBS for a wastewater plant.[4] Although some WBS elements are not shown (such as any cross-cutting elements), the WBS is consistent with the principles discussed in this book. The reason is that both the design phase and the construction phase have specific and different output products or deliverables at the end of each phase and do not represent organizations working on the same product elements. Each phase represents different work with different output products and meets the *PMBOK® Guide* definition of a phase: *A collection of logically-related project activities, usually culminating in the completion of a major deliverable.*[5]

On the other hand, Figure 3-10 is the representation of a WBS that is incorrectly organized. The problem is that the Level 2 items: *product requirements—detail design—construct—integration and test* are not phases, but work packages. The Level 3 elements of each of these are identical and are really the primary output products of the project.

In general, whenever a WBS is presented with all the next level elements identical, the WBS should be reviewed to see if an orthogonal presentation would be more representative of the product breakdown. The exception is some situations where a generic breakdown is used as a template and the user is expected to select the appropriate elements from the suite of possible elements. The preferred WBS for Software Product Release 5.0 is shown in

FIGURE 3-9   Partial Program WBS—Wastewater Plant

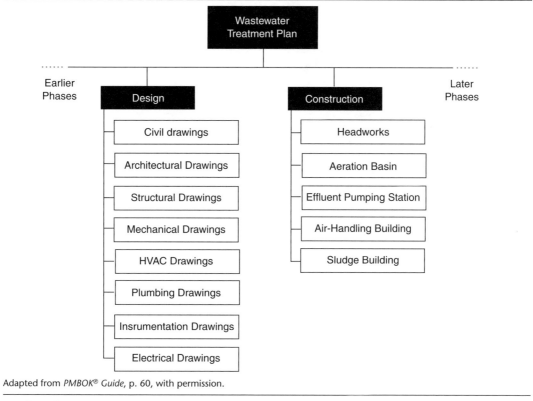

Adapted from *PMBOK® Guide*, p. 60, with permission.

FIGURE 3-10   Incorrectly Organized WBS

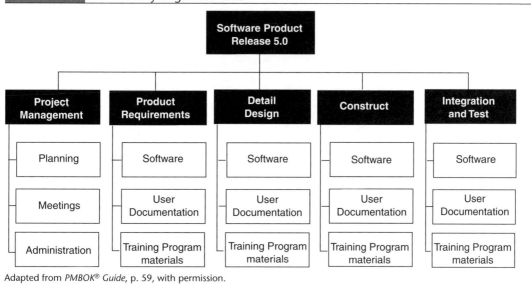

Adapted from *PMBOK® Guide*, p. 59, with permission.

Figure 3-11. In the preferred version, it was necessary to change the names of some of the WBS elements to be consistent with the work to be performed.

Focusing on the output products—software, user documentation, and training program materials—results in a much more coherent WBS with the work packages at the lowest level of the WBS.

The work breakdown structure is used to organize and define the work in projects. However, all projects have phases and a project lifecycle; as projects get larger in size, these phases become significant and require planning in and of themselves. Programs consist of a set of projects, usually with an element of ongoing activity. A program WBS needs to be developed for these larger projects to be able to integrate the planning of the projects. The program WBS may have a program management element at the first level as well as project management elements in each of the next level projects.

FIGURE 3-11   Sample WBS Organized by Output Product—Preferred WBS

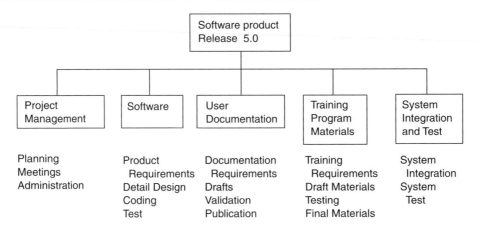

NOTES

1. Project Management Institute Standards Committee, *A Guide to the Project Management Body of Knowledge* (Upper Darby, PA: Project Management Institute, 2000), p.14.
2. Ibid., p. 205.
3. Department of Defense, MIL-STD-881 *Work Breakdown Structures for Defense Materiel Items*, Sections 2.1 and 2.2 (Washington D.C.: Headquarters, Air Force Systems Command, Directorate of Cost Analysis, 1 November 1968).
4. *PMBOK® Guide*, p. 60.
5. Ibid., *Guide*, p. 205.

CHAPTER 4

The WBS in Project Operations

The WBS can be used in each of the nine project management knowledge areas described in the *PMBOK® Guide.*[1]

SCOPE MANAGEMENT

Scope management includes the processes required to ensure that the project scope includes all the work required—and only the work required—to complete the project successfully.[2] Many tools used for scope management involve the WBS.

Project Charter

The *project charter* is one of the primary documents used to define a project, its objectives, and outputs, and to establish the general framework for its implementation. A commonly used variant, the *project manager's charter*, serves as the contract between the project manager and the project sponsor and establishes the parameters of the assignment, including resources and authority. It usually is prepared following an authorization to spend resources on a project and may include a statement of work.

The project manager prepares the document; it is then reviewed and approved by senior management and, in some cases, the customer. In a matrix organization, the supporting organizations must concur as well. Charters vary in size and comprehensiveness depending on the size of the project and usually vary from three to ten pages in length. For small projects, the project charter may be a verbal agreement; however, the project manager should document the agreement for his or her own reference.

The paragraphs and sections within a project charter may vary from project to project, but the major areas addressed are shown in the outline in Figure 4-1. The outline needs to be tailored to the project and the project environment. The charter should include all the information and guidance needed to acquire resources and begin development of the WBS and detailed project planning. For the purposes of this text, the important contents are

FIGURE 4-1   Outline of the Project Charter

Project Purpose
Project Objectives

Summary Project Description
- General Description of the Work
- *Description of the End Products, Services, or Results* and Expected Quality or Performance
- Schedule and Budget
- Resources to Be Provided

Project Manager
- Authority
- Responsibility
- Coordination Requirements
- Reporting Requirements

Facilities and Environment
Supporting Activities/Organizations
- Resources to Be Supplied

Customer and Customer Relations
Transfer or Delivery of the End Products, Services, or Results
Final Acceptance Criteria

the deliverable products, services, or results since this information provides the basis for development of the WBS.

The WBS provides the outline of the written statement of work or scope statement and also the framework for related items used to characterize the project.

Statement of Work

The statement of work (SOW) is a document that describes in clear, understandable terms what project work is to be accomplished, what products are to be delivered, and what services are to be performed. Preparation of an effective statement of work requires a thorough understanding of the products and services needed to satisfy a particular requirement. Because the WBS is established based on work performed to deliver the end items, the WBS is used for the outline of the SOW. The WBS dictionary with minor modifications can readily be converted into SOW language for a contract document. A statement of work expressed in explicit terms will facilitate effective communications during the planning phase and effective project evaluation during the implementation phase, when the SOW becomes the standard for measuring project performance.

Using a standardized WBS as a template when constructing the statement of work for a project helps streamline the process. Using the WBS also facilitates a logical arrangement of the SOW elements, provides a convenient checklist to ensure that all necessary elements of the project are addressed, and directs the project to meet specific contract reporting or data deliverable needs.

TIME MANAGEMENT

The WBS is used as the framework for planning and scheduling. Using project management software or scheduling forms, the process is shown in Figure 4-2.

Figure 4-3 illustrates the WBS of the example in Chapter 2 in the section, Use of the WBS to Develop Activities, and was entered into Microsoft Project 98.® The WBS is used as the primary input to activity definition: Step 1 of the process list of Figure 4-2. Figure 4-4 illustrates the same WBS but with the identification of the deliverables added as zero duration activities. Figure 4-5 represents the final schedule after the activities and their durations are

FIGURE 4-2   Schedule Development Process

Starting with the WBS:
1. Enter the WBS into the Project Management software package.
2. List all deliverable end items or services under their appropriate WBS element; identify the required schedule date, if applicable.
3. Define and list activities under each lowest-level WBS element (i.e. the work package); establish activity durations and, if applicable, activity resources.
4. Identify predecessor—successor relationships between activities.
5. Iterate steps 2—3 as necessary to achieve a workable schedule.

FIGURE 4-3 Step 1 of the Scheduling Process

TIME SHARING SYSTEM (TSS) PROJECT

ID	WBS	Task Name	January 12/30	01/06	01/13	01/20	01/27	February 02/03	02/10	02/17
1	1	**TSS REQUIREMENTS SPECIFICATION**	▼							
2	1.1	INITIAL TSS REQUIREMENTS SPECIFICATION	▪							
3	1.2	FINAL TSS REQUIREMENTS SPECIFICATION	◆ 01/02							
4	2	**TSS DESIGN SPECIFICATION**	▼							
5	2.1	INITIAL TSS DESIGN SPECIFICATION	▪							
6	2.2	FINAL TSS DESIGN SPECIFICATION	◆ 01/02							
7	3	**TSS SOFTWARE**	▼							
8	3.1	TSS MODULE 1	▬							
9	3.2	TSS MODULE 2	▬							

added and the activities are linked. The process is logical, orderly, and easy once the WBS is completed.

The results of Steps 3 and 4 are illustrated in the completed schedule in Figure 4-5. The activities identified in Chapter 2 have been added and linked, identifying the predecessors and successors. (See Figure 2-14 for the final schedule, including the addition of project management activities.)

FIGURE 4-4 Step 2 of the Scheduling Process—Add Deliverables

TIME SHARING SYSTEM (TSS) PROJECT

ID	WBS	Task Name	January 12/30	01/06	01/13	01/20	01/27	February 02/03	02/10	02/17
1	1	**TSS REQUIREMENTS SPECIFICATION**	▼							
2	1.1	INITIAL TSS REQUIREMENTS SPECIFICATION	▪							
3	1.2	**FINAL TSS REQUIREMENTS SPECIFICATION**	◆ 01/02							
4	1.2.1	Deliver TSS Requirements Specification	◆ 01/02							
5	2	**TSS DESIGN SPECIFICATION**	▼							
6	2.1	INITIAL TSS DESIGN SPECIFICATION	▪							
7	2.2	**FINAL TSS DESIGN SPECIFICATION**	◆ 01/02							
8	2.2.1	Deliver TSS Design Specification	◆ 01/02							
9	3	**TSS SOFTWARE**	▼							
10	3.1	TSS MODULE 1	▬							
11	3.2	TSS MODULE 2	▬							
12	3.3	**INTEGRATE MODULES**	◆ 01/02							
13	3.3.1	Complete TSS Software	◆ 01/02							

FIGURE 4-5 Completion of Steps 3 and 4 of the Scheduling Process

TIME SHARING SYSTEM (TSS) PROJECT

ID	WBS	Task Name	Duration	Timeline
1	1	**TSS REQUIREMENTS SPECIFICATION**	**10 days**	
2	**1.1**	**INITIAL TSS REQUIREMENTS SPECIFICATION**	**10 days**	
3	1.1.1	Create Initial TSS Rqmts Spec	5 days	
4	1.1.2	Review Initial TSS Reqmts Spec	2 days	
5	1.1.3	Update Initial TSS Reqmts Spec	3 days	
6	**1.2**	**FINAL TSS REQUIREMENTS SPECIFICATION**	**3 days**	
7	1.2.1	Review Final TSS Reqmts Spec	2 days	
8	1.2.2	Approve Final TSS Reqmts Spec	1 day	
9	1.2.3	Deliver TSS Requirements Specification	0 days	01/15
10	2	**TSS DESIGN SPECIFICATION**	**17 days**	
11	**2.1**	**INITIAL TSS DESIGN SPECIFICATION**	**13 days**	
12	2.1.1	Create Initial TSS Design Spec	7 days	
13	2.1.2	Review Initial TSS Design Spec	3 days	
14	2.1.3	Update Initial TSS Design Spec	3 days	
15	**2.2**	**FINAL TSS DESIGN SPECIFICATION**	**4 days**	
16	2.2.1	Review Final TSS Design Spec	2 days	
17	2.2.2	Approve Final TSS Design Spec	2 days	
18	2.2.3	Deliver TSS Design Specification	0 days	02/04
19	3	**TSS SOFTWARE**	**25 days**	
20	**3.1**	**TSS MODULE 1**	**20 days**	
21	3.1.1	Code TSS Module 1	15 days	
22	3.1.2	Unit Test TSS Module 1	5 days	
23	**3.2**	**TSS MODULE 2**	**20 days**	
24	3.2.1	Code TSS Module 2	15 days	
25	3.2.2	Unit Test TSS Module 2	5 days	
26	**3.3**	**INTEGRATE MODULES**	**5 days**	
27	3.3.1	System Test Integrated Modules	5 days	
28	3.3.2	Complete TSS Software	0 days	

Timeline column headers: January (2/3, 1/0, 1/1, 1/2), 1/2, February (2/0, 2/1, 2/1), 2/2, March (3/0, 3/1)

Experience shows that once the WBS is entered into the software in the Gantt chart format, the activity definition actually can be performed faster than most people can type the descriptive activity names. Duration information, resource information, and linkages do not need to be performed in any particular order, and often are performed concurrently with activity definition. The important step is to get the complete WBS entered into the computer program down to the work package level; then the rest of the activity definition proceeds rapidly and comprehensively. Experience also shows that revisions to the WBS occur in this process as activities are defined.

COST MANAGEMENT

There are five special applications of the WBS in cost management:
1. Bottom-up cost estimation
2. Collection of historical data
3. Chart of accounts linkage
4. Earned value management system implementation
5. Budgeting.

Bottom-Up Cost Estimation

Bottom-up cost estimation is the most commonly used technique for estimating the total cost of a project. As the name implies, it is a summation of the estimated cost of all the activities or work packages of the project. The WBS is normally used as the framework for preparing the initial comprehensive estimate and subsequent budgets.

The estimation process is relatively simple; each activity is identified as discussed under Time Management, and the responsible person or organization is asked to provide an estimate of the work to be performed. These activity-level estimates are collected and summed to provide the total project estimate. On larger projects, work packages or cost accounts are used as the building blocks for the cost estimate.

Figure 4-6 is an example of a typical form used to collect work package data by WBS descriptor for bottom-up estimation. The same form, with minor modification, can be used for activity-level estimating. It is the comprehensiveness of a properly developed WBS that ensures that all costs are included. This form is then used to enter the data into the computer system. Alternately, of course, experienced personnel may enter these data directly into the computer during the scheduling process.

Collection of Historical Data

One of the purposes of the Department of Defense's *Work Breakdown Structures for Defense Materiel Items* was to collect data for the seven types of military systems in a common framework. To achieve this, the use of a specified WBS was required for the first three levels of each system. "Using

FIGURE 4-6   Sample Work Package Cost Estimating Form

WORK PACKAGE COST ESTIMATION FORM

Project Name: _____

WBS:_____ Title: _____Organization Code: _____

Scheduled Start: _____ Estimated Duration: _____ Workdays

Person Hours per Day

Resource Name										Total Hours

Travel:
Origin:_____ Destination:_____ No. of Days: _____

No. of Persons: _____ Purpose: _____

Other Direct Costs: _____

Consultant Dollars: _____ Materials: _____

Notes and Explanation:

Approved:	Date:	Approved:	Date:

available data to build historic files to aid in the future development of similar defense materiel items is a very valuable resource."[3] Definitions are included (a WBS dictionary) of each Level 1-3 WBS element, which further assists in ensuring that interpretations of the content of each element are consistent from project to project.

In many organizations, the products and projects are similar—for example, an engineering firm that specializes in designing and constructing highway bridges or a software firm that specializes in relational data bases. It is to their advantage to develop standard WBS structures and templates, at least at the top levels, to be able to collect historical cost data and perhaps other data as well. These data can then be used to assist in the cost estimation activity for new projects in the feasibility phases and to provide an initial top-down estimate for any new proposed similar project. More sophisticated organizations are able to develop cost estimating relations (CERs) using multiple regression techniques.

Chart of Accounts Linkage

The chart of accounts maintained by the accounting organization does not normally relate directly to the WBS. The WBS is output-oriented, and the chart of accounts identifies expense or cost categories that are inputs to the organization. Typical examples are labor, material, and other direct cost accounts. For cost management, the project manager needs a capability to relate the various categories of labor, material, and direct cost items to the appropriate project, cost account, and/or work package for proper allocation of incurred costs. The extent of the linkage depends on the need to control project costs, the level of control required, and the capability of the accounting system.

Earned Value Management System Implementation

Earned value management (EVM) systems require a detailed WBS and a close relationship between the WBS and the accounting system at the work package level. Ordinarily, cost accounts are established at the lowest level of the WBS at which actual costs are collected and compared to budgeted costs for particular organizations. Within cost accounts, work packages are identified, planned, and budgeted.

When implementing an EVM system, the organization must formulate and determine status on a monthly basis for each cost account established in the WBS.

Four types of data required for earned value/performance measurement are:

1. Budgeted Costs for Work Scheduled (BWCS)—the planned value
2. Actual Costs for Work Performed (ACWP)—actual costs
3. Budgeted Costs for Work Performed (BCWP)—earned value
4. Estimate at Completion (EAC).[4]

The primary report used for analysis of performance in an EVM system is called the cost/schedule status report. It includes these four types of data in addition to calculated cost and schedule variance data *for each WBS element* from the cost account level up to total project level.

Budgeting

Just as cost estimates are prepared using the WBS as the framework, budgets are similarly developed and coordinated. Budgets are planned and issued to organizations using work authorization forms, as discussed earlier. Budgets then become part of the cost baseline for measuring performance.

COMMUNICATIONS

The WBS provides the framework for identifying and organizing the communications mechanisms used on a project. Discussions of the project, parts of the project, and explanations of project work are facilitated when the WBS is used as an outline to identify the topic under discussion and relate the particular WBS element to the work as a whole. All reporting requirements for the project should be consistent with the WBS and WBS numbering system. It is common for customers or sponsors to require progress reports to be structured by WBS Level 2 or 3 elements.

Project reviews are frequently structured with discussions of specific WBS elements and, since most cost and schedule reports relate to WBS elements, it is a common framework. The other framework is the organizational breakdown structure (OBS). Action item and issue tracking systems frequently use the WBS number as one of the data elements to sort and relate the open items to specific deliverables.

Project correspondence also is expected to refer to WBS numbers when discussing areas of project work, and correspondence reference numbers frequently are WBS-based. Correspondence tracking systems have a WBS field for organizing correspondence. Filing systems consist of a day file for copies filed by date and a subject file using the WBS number where applicable. On large complex projects, the contract line items, configuration items, contract statement of work tasks, contract specifications, technical and management reports, and potential subcontractor responses are all related to the WBS numbering system.

For purposes of team building and developing an accurate WBS, the WBS development should be a team effort. The advantages are team discussion of all elements as well as improved understanding of the work to be done and where each individual fits within the overall project. Some geographically dispersed organizations use videoconferencing techniques to develop the WBS for new projects and, thereby, receive input from the most experienced persons company-wide.

PROCUREMENT MANAGEMENT

When a product or service is procured or outsourced, the customer usually provides the top-level WBS for the product or service in the request for proposal (RFP). One reason is that different bidders use the same framework for planning, cost estimating, and responding to the RFP, facilitating the evaluation and source selection process. If only a part of the project is to be outsourced, it usually is a discrete work package from the project WBS. For example, a project for building a house could have the HVAC system as a discrete element that is clearly identified and easily defined. The WBS facilitates communication and simplifies the planning and control on a large project where many work elements may be subcontracted.

The individual WBS element or elements from the project WBS that apply to a proposed subcontract are selected by the project manager for inclusion in a draft RFP. This is the initial time for open dialogue between the customer and potential contractors. Innovative ideas or alternative solutions are collected for inclusion in the final WBS and RFP, which includes a subcontract WBS and the initial WBS dictionary for the procured item or service. The RFP instructs potential contractors to extend the selected subcontract WBS elements to define the complete subcontract scope.

Contractors extend the subcontract WBS to the level that satisfies the critical visibility requirements and does not overburden the management control system. They submit the complete subcontract WBS with their proposal. The proposal should be based on the WBS in the RFP, although contractors may suggest changes needed to meet an essential requirement of the RFP or to enhance the effectiveness of the subcontract WBS in satisfying program objectives.

QUALITY AND TECHNICAL PERFORMANCE MANAGEMENT

There is limited interaction between project quality and technical performance management and the WBS, except to use the WBS element identification system to communicate areas of the project where there are quality or technical performance interests.

An exception is the numbering system used for a specification tree on some larger, complex systems projects. A specification tree structures the performance parameters for the system or systems being developed into a series or hierarchy of specifications. It subdivides the system into its component elements and identifies the performance objectives of the system and its elements. The performance characteristics are explicitly identified and quantified. This subdivision is the same as the decomposition in the product WBS.

The completed specification tree represents a hierarchy of performance requirements for each component element of the system for which design responsibility is assigned. The WBS numbering usually identifies the elements where performance specifications are required. Because specifications may not be written for each element of the WBS, the specification tree usually maps only the product-related elements of the WBS.

HUMAN RESOURCE MANAGEMENT

Project human resource management includes the processes required to make the most effective use of the people involved in the project.[5] As such, there is limited interface with the WBS.

Development of an effective WBS is not as straightforward as it first appears. For example, in Chapter 2, alternate WBS structures are discussed and in many chapters information is provided on the preferred approach to preparing a WBS. A major obstacle in organizations is the culture of the organization, especially if organization and input-oriented WBSs have become common. Organizations develop a certain way of doing business, and changes—even obvious improvements—are not always easy to accomplish. Strategies such as those discussed by Kotter are necessary to introduce changes in cultures.[6]

One of the best methods to start building a project team is to use the development of the initial project WBS as the vehicle. This has three advantages:

1. The new team quickly becomes involved in defining the project and project scope and, therefore, internalizes the project.
2. The expertise of the team is used to help ensure that all the work that needs to be performed is represented in the WBS—in other words, that the WBS is complete.
3. The WBS becomes the framework for communicating information concerning the project.

The resource assignment matrix is one of the tools used to plan the use of human resources. It is a cross-referencing of organization versus WBS and work package to show who is responsible for specific assignments on a project and the specific type of responsibility, such as performance, approval, reviewing, and coordination.

RISK MANAGEMENT

Project risk management is the systematic process of identifying, analyzing, and responding to project risk; the WBS provides a logical structure for this process.[7] There are two areas where the WBS is important in project risk management. The first is an input to risk management planning where the WBS is used as a tool in the development of the risk management plan. This plan describes how risk identification, qualitative and quantitative analysis, response planning, monitoring, and control are structured and performed during the project lifecycle. The role of the WBS is to provide a roadmap to the elements that involve project risk.

The second area is the use of the WBS as an input to the risk identification process. The WBS is used as a checklist of all the work areas of the project to identify possible risks that require analysis and monitoring. Various techniques for qualitative risk analysis are described generically in the *PMBOK® Guide*.[8] One method involves using the WBS as the framework and identifying the risk probability of selected elements and the impact on the project of the same elements. The products of these two factors are ranked to determine the higher risk areas.

This qualitative approach for assessing risk can be used for any type of project: simple, complex, small, or large, and product, service, or result. Leading the team through the process builds understanding of potential problems and agreement about team response.

PROJECT INTEGRATION MANAGEMENT

Project integration management is defined in the *PMBOK® Guide* to include the processes required to ensure that the various elements of the project are properly coordinated.[9] The WBS is an obvious tool to assist in this function. There are two aspects of this *PMBOK® Guide* knowledge area that involve the WBS: (1) the project plan, and (2) configuration management.

Project Plan

The project plan is a document used to guide both project execution and project control. A WBS defined to the level at which management control is exercised is included as a baseline document within the project plan. Figure 4-7 is an example of a sample outline for a project plan. Based on the project plan, a work authorization system, using the WBS numbering scheme to reference the relevant work, is used to sanction project work.

FIGURE 4-7   Sample Project Plan Outline

I. Project Summary
II. Scope Statement
    A. Project Justification
    B. Project Objectives
    C. Assumptions
    D. Critical Success Factors
    E. Major Milestones
III. **Work Breakdown Structure**
IV. Project Schedule
V. Detail Work Plan
VI. Resource Plan
VII. Risk Management Plan
VIII. Quality Plan
IX. Communication Plan
X. Change Management Plan
XI. Project Tracking and Control
XII. Project Close-Out

Configuration Management

Configuration management is the process of managing the technical configuration of items being developed whose requirements are specified, and managing the scope of the project. Deliverable items are designated in the WBS, the schedule, the statement of work, and/or other project documents.

Configuration management involves defining the baseline configuration for the configuration items, controlling the changes to that baseline, and accounting for all approved changes. In establishing the requirement for configuration management on a project, the project manager needs to designate which deliverables are subject to configuration management controls and the documents that formally describe them. When working on a contract, usually all deliverables are controlled. A contract deliverable designated for configuration management is called a configuration item. For software, this item is commonly called a computer software configuration item (CSCI).

In addition to deliverables, the contract statement of work and the WBS are subject to configuration management to control proposed changes that impact them. The WBS and WBS dictionary, scope statement, or statement of work are the documents that define the scope of the project. When the WBS is defined, and the project team and customer or sponsor agree that it is complete, it becomes part of the total baseline for the project. Work not covered by the WBS is not part of the project.

To add work to the project is to change scope. The project should use a formal process of change management to modify the WBS and supporting documents by adding or deleting work in the statement of work and changing project schedules and budgets accordingly. The WBS then becomes a major tool for controlling the phenomenon known as *scope creep*. Scope creep arises from unfunded, informal additions to the project work. Abramovici advises: "Controlling scope creep is one of the project manager's major tasks, and he or she has to start working on it even before the project statement of work is written."[10]

When a request for a change is received, either formally or informally, a first step in the analysis is to determine whether or not the change affects the scope of the project. If the work to be performed is covered by the WBS and described in the WBS dictionary or the statement of work, then it is in scope. Otherwise, the work is out of scope. In that event, the project manager must formally evaluate the impact of the change on cost, schedule, and technical performance, and make the necessary changes to contractual documents and plans to implement the change, if it is approved.

The WBS is a useful tool in each of the nine project management knowledge areas of the *PMBOK® Guide*. It provides a framework for interrelating all the project management functions to specific work areas of the project.

NOTES

1. Project Management Institute Standards Committee, *A Guide to the Project Management Body of Knowledge* (Upper Darby, PA: Project Management Institute, 2000), p.40.
2. Ibid., p. 51.
3. Department of Defense, MIL-STD-881 *Work Breakdown Structures for Defense Materiel Items* (Washington D.C.: Headquarters, Air Force Systems Command, Directorate of Cost Analysis, 1 November 1968), Section 1.4.3.
4. Q.W. Fleming, *Put Earned Value (C/SCSC) into Your Management Control System* (Worthington, OH: Publishing Horizons, Inc., 1983), p.52.
5. *PMBOK® Guide*, p. 107.
6. J. P. Kotter, *Leading Change* (Boston: Harvard Business School Press, 1996).
7. *PMBOK® Guide*, p.127.
8. Ibid., p. 135.
9. Ibid., p. 41.
10. A. Abramovici, "Controlling Scope Creep," *PM Network* (January 2000), 44-48.

CHAPTER 5

WBS Examples and Descriptions

This chapter presents and analyzes examples of different types of work breakdown structures (WBSs) that are analyzed to illustrate how the principles presented in this book apply universally. They complement the examples presented in earlier chapters for relatively simple projects.

The examples include the following five projects:

1. Implementation of a new management philosophy
2. Cross-cultural and cross-border challenge resolution
3. Book writing project
4. Dinner party project
5. Museum project (project definition phase).

EXAMPLE 1—WBS FOR IMPLEMENTATION OF A NEW ORGANIZATION-WIDE MANAGEMENT PHILOSOPHY

Figure 5-1 is an example of a WBS that represents the work required to implement enterprise project management (EPM) throughout an organization. The WBS was developed by Dinsmore and is presented here as an example of this application.[1]

Dinsmore states: "A holistic view is required to chart the pathway to successfully implement enterprise project management, and it all starts with the work breakdown structure."[2]

The Level 2 WBS elements as defined by Dinsmore are as follows:

1. **Management of the PM Program**—work covering the key elements for managing the EPM program to ensure that adequate managerial effort is focused on the program.
2. **Strategic Alignment with Company Objectives**—work performed to ensure that projects are aligned with company objectives.
3. **Cultural Change**—work performed to change the way of doing business.
4. **Communication**—work areas necessary for communicating strategies and developing awareness of the changes.

FIGURE 5-1 Details WBS—EPM Project

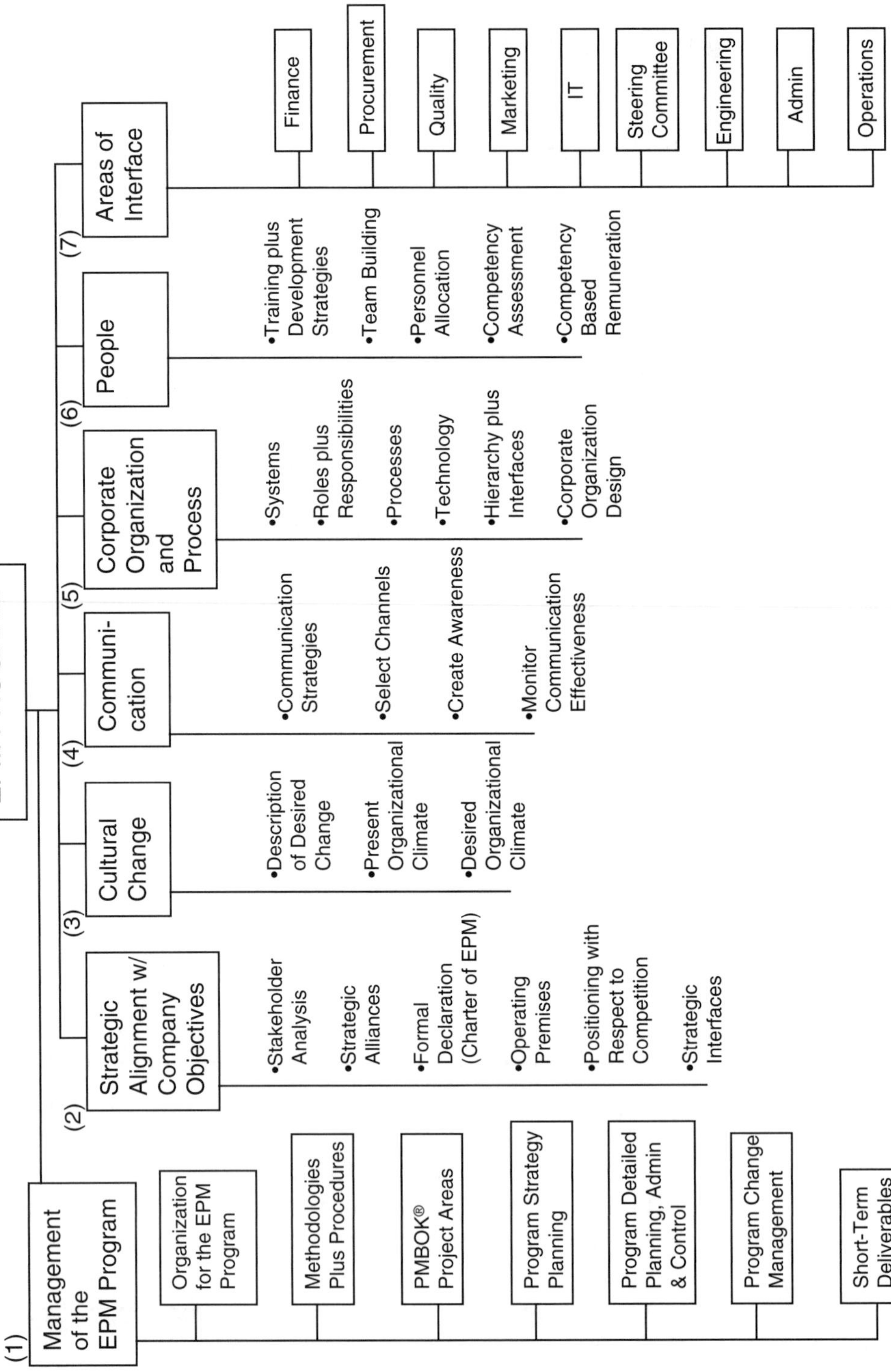

EPM PROGRAM

(1) Management of the EPM Program
- Organization for the EPM Program
- Methodologies Plus Procedures
- PMBOK® Project Areas
- Program Strategy Planning
- Program Detailed Planning, Admin & Control
- Program Change Management
- Short-Term Deliverables

(2) Strategic Alignment w/ Company Objectives
- Stakeholder Analysis
- Strategic Alliances
- Formal Declaration (Charter of EPM)
- Operating Premises
- Positioning with Respect to Competition
- Strategic Interfaces

(3) Cultural Change
- Description of Desired Change
- Present Organizational Climate
- Desired Organizational Climate

(4) Communication
- Communication Strategies
- Select Channels
- Create Awareness
- Monitor Communication Effectiveness

(5) Corporate Organization and Process
- Systems
- Roles plus Responsibilities
- Processes
- Technology
- Hierarchy plus Interfaces
- Corporate Organization Design

(6) People
- Training plus Development Strategies
- Team Building
- Personnel Allocation
- Competency Assessment
- Competency Based Remuneration

(7) Areas of Interface
- Finance
- Procurement
- Quality
- Marketing
- IT
- Steering Committee
- Engineering
- Admin
- Operations

5. **Corporate Organization and Process**—work involved in making adjustments across the organization and changing processes.

6. **People**—work related to people issues.

7. **Areas of Interface**—work related to specific functional areas where there is an interface with EPM.

In the context of the anatomy of a WBS, this is a service project with the objectives to be attained represented by WBS elements in four primary areas:

1. Strategic alignment
2. Cultural change
3. Corporate organization and process
4. People.

Each of these has deliverables or outputs that collectively produce the final product: a documented and integrated EPM system that is internalized in the organization.

There are two cross-cutting elements: *communication* and *areas of interface*. The communication element is *analytical* since it spans the other work elements and produces outputs based on that analysis. The elements under areas of interface are *integrative* since they represent the work involved in putting together the work in the other elements into the nine functional areas listed as Level 3.

The last WBS element, *management of the EPM program*, is the normal project management element that identifies the managerial responsibilities and activities of the project management office.

EXAMPLE 2—WBS FOR CROSS-CULTURAL AND CROSS-BORDER CHALLENGES

International projects frequently face difficulties because of the differences in cultures, laws, expectations, and communications. Everyone does not think or manage in the style used by Americans. Grove, Hallowell, and Smith recommend developing a parallel WBS for international projects that, in effect, is a project within a project. The objective is to manage the project's international dimension to minimize the impact on the principal project.[3]

The unusual feature is the format of the WBS descriptions. The WBS for this project is presented in Figure 5-2.

This WBS appears to be in "activity" format, but actually includes part of the WBS dictionary in each WBS element. The Level 3 elements are work packages, which describe "what" is to be accomplished in each element. The

FIGURE 5-2 Sample WBS with Activity-like Descriptors

WBS FOR CROSS-CULTURAL AND CROSS-BORDER CHALLENGES PROJECT

1. "Culture Risk Management (CRM) Team" Identified, Assigned, Funded, Charged

1.1 Responsibilities of "CRM Team" specified (see 2 through 9 below)
1.2 Structural and functional location of CRM team in project unit addressed
1.2.1 Budget and charge number allocated; reporting relationships determined
1.2.2 Manager and members' assignment conditions, rotations, determined
1.2.3 Formal status reports from CRM team: timing and dissemination planned

2. Cross-Cultural and Cross-Border Information Collected
2.1 Identify means of collecting relevant information
2.1.1 Existing means within firm: HR, T&D, library, legal department, etc,
2.1.2 Published materials: books, journal and magazine articles, web sites
2.1.3 Informants: host nationals, "old hands," cross-cultural consultants
2.2 Collect and catalog relevant information
2.2.1 Business, regulatory, legal, international trade
2.2.2 Religion, family, education, economics, politics, etc.
2.2.3 Work relationships and work styles, incentives, communication, decision-making, etc,
2.2.4 Technology transfer issues related to local trainees and larger society
2.3 Study and evaluate the most relevant collected information
2.4 Disseminate selected information across entire project team, translating if necessary

3. Project Plans and Company Business Practices Risk-Assessed
3.1 Assess cross-cultural/border risks in project objectives, WBS, budget, timeline
3.2 Assess risks in company's business, quality, personnel practices when applied abroad
3.3 Prepare a formal risk assessment statement

4. Strategy Developed, Recommendations to Project Manager Delivered
4.1 Develop strategies, including specific WBS, for avoiding/reducing major perceived risks
4.2 Recommend specific risk-reduction strategies to senior management

5. Foreign Project Personnel Oriented and Supported
5.1 Determine difficulties commonly faced by foreign assignees at project site(s)
5.2 Determine sources of cooperation and aid within, and external to, the company
5.3 Develop and deliver supportive services to assignees directly or via consultants
5.3.1 Create and distribute orientation handbook
5.3.2 Deal first-hand with assignees' practical relocation and settling-in concerns
5.3.3 Provide pre-departure and in-country cultural coaching and language training
5.3.4 Develop procedures for health/safety, R&R, crisis support, emergencies

6. Host National, Foreign Assignee, Home-Office Personnel Integrated

6.1 Compare work style and work relationship patterns of foreigners and host nationals
6.2 Assess home-office/field-site relationships and communication hurdles
6.3 Compare social and entertainment traditions of foreign and host cultures
6.4 Develop working arrangements and events to gradually integrate different groups
6.4.1 Work style and colleague relationship expectations, reporting arrangements
6.4.2 Home-office / field-site relationship, communication facilitation
6.4.3 Welcoming events for newcomers; milestone events to celebrate successes
6.4.4 Social and holiday events drawing on different cultural groups' traditions

7. Cross-Cultural and Cross-Border Training Delivered
7.1 Determine pressing cross-cultural and cross-border concerns of project personnel
7.2 Compare training and education traditions of foreign and host cultures
7.3 Develop and deliver training and/or coaching for project personnel

8. Culture-Conflict Damage Containment Strategy Developed
8.1 Predict most likely cross-cultural conflict/ misunderstanding situations
8.2 Develop strategies for CRM team's response to ameliorate conflicts

9. Organizational Learning Based on CRM Team's Experience Realized
9.1 Include cross-border/cultural risk reduction in quality
9.2 Prepare and periodically disseminate CRM team formal status reports
9.3 Rotate high-potential personnel as Culture Risk Manager and CRM team members
9.4 Debrief by senior policy-makers of manager and team members
9.5 Disseminate widely a summary report of CRM overall effort

Reprinted with permission from C. Grove, W. Hallowell, and C. Smith, "A Parallel WBS for International Projects," *PM Network®* (March 1999), 37–42.

true activities are at Levels 4 and 5. Since a successful project was described, the WBS clearly served its purpose.

There are several major areas with output products or results to be attained. These are the development of project risk assessments and strategies, the orientation and support of foreign project personnel, the integration of host national, foreign assignee, and home-office personnel, the delivery of cross-cultural and cross-border training, and the development of damage containment strategy. It is important that the developers of the WBS of this complexity be assured that the 100 percent rule is followed.

In the cross-cutting area, the *information collection* is analytical and provides input to many of the other areas. The cross-cutting project management element is in two parts: *the CRM team identified, assigned, funded, charged* element; and the *organizational learning* element.

An alternate WBS for the same project could be structured as shown in Figure 5-3. The numbers above each Level 2 WBS element correspond to the WBS elements from the original version that would be moved or combined into this element to simplify the WBS and group like items. The *research and information* element is a cross-cutting *analytic* element, and the *project risk* and *personnel* elements provide the basis for the product breakdown of the primary deliverables. The *project risk* element outputs relate to the impact of the cross-cultural and cross-border elements on the primary project work. The *personnel* element outputs relate to the products, services, and results

FIGURE 5-3   Alternate WBS for Cross-Cultural and Cross-Border Project

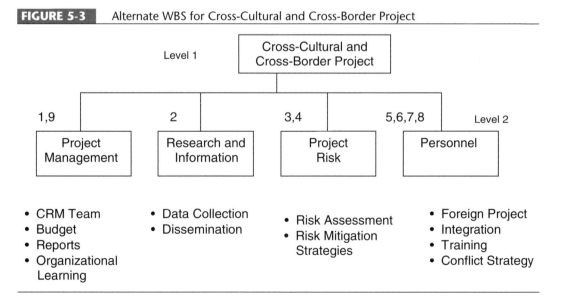

planned for the foreign project personnel, host national, and home office personnel.

EXAMPLE 3—WBS FOR A BOOK WRITING PROJECT

Writing a book or preparing a report where research is required is a common activity. There is a tendency to identify the research or the writing as the primary output, when the primary product is the actual published book. This sample in Figure 5-4 is included to provide more detail than was included in the example used earlier.

The *research* element is both an analytical element and a process element. The *writing* element is a process element representing the writing phase of the project. Once the writing is complete and the chapters edited, the next and final phase of publishing the book proceeds. Note that the Level 2 *research* element generally covers the work that applies to the book as a whole and the *research* work packages at Level 4 relate to chapter-specific research.

EXAMPLE 4—WBS FOR A DINNER PARTY PROJECT

The dinner party project in Figure 5-5 is a service-type project. Project management is the only cross-cutting element at Level 2. This WBS was initially prepared from the bottom-up by first listing all the activities as shown, and then grouping them into the logical categories as shown at Level 2.

This WBS contains work elements at Level 1 and 2 and activities at Level 3. Note that food and drink could be separated at Level 3 and the activities under each would be at Level 4. Similarly, the house category could be separated into work areas related to cleaning and the dinner environment. There is no logic in the order of the activities listed under each WBS element.

A top-down WBS would have been structured as shown in Figure 5-6, where the initial focus would be on the objectives and outputs. The primary output is the actual dinner and other outputs are the invitation activities and house preparation. In any event, the WBS elements, except for project management, are service elements and represent the logical grouping of activities to facilitate planning.

A WBS for a service project, where there is not a tangible product, does not usually have any cross-cutting elements except for project management. The reason is that there is usually a main event, like the dinner itself, but there is no inherent physical structure to the elements, only a logical grouping. The other elements are also convenient and logical categories of work that

FIGURE 5-4 Sample Book Writing Project

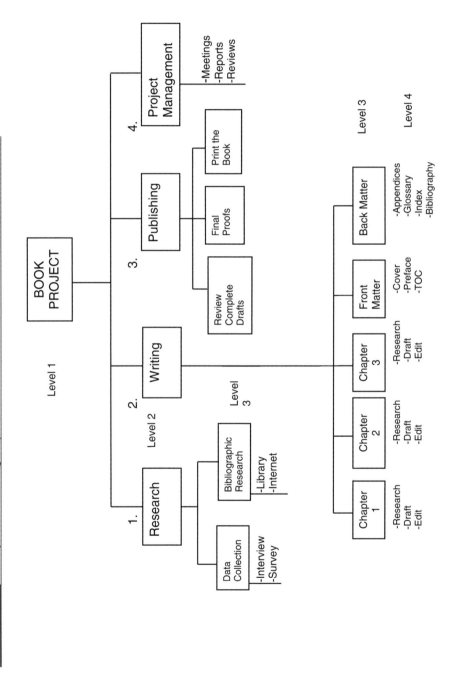

FIGURE 5-5   Bottom-Up WBS for a Dinner Party

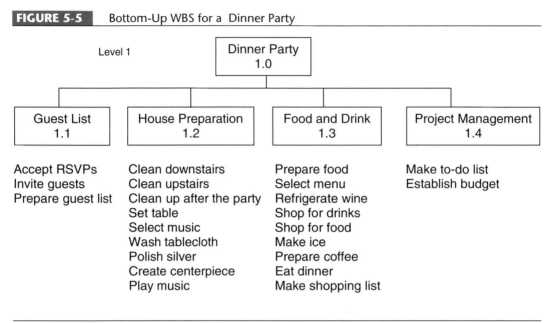

complement the main event.

EXAMPLE 5—WBS FOR A MUSEUM EXHIBIT PROJECT (PROJECT DEFINITION PHASE)

Figure 5-7 is an illustration of a WBS for the project definition phase of the museum exhibit program outlined in Figures 3-4 through 3-7. This WBS

FIGURE 5-6   Top-Down WBS for Dinner Party

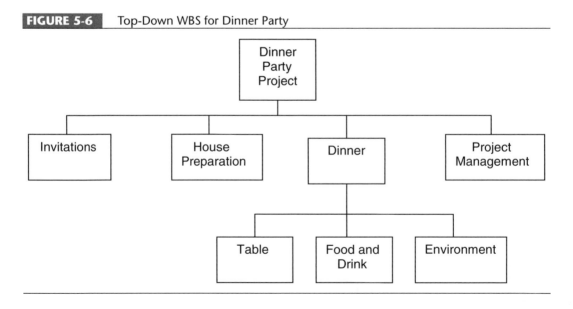

FIGURE 5-7   Museum Exhibit Program—Program Definition Phase WBS

A.1 Concept and Content Development
    A.1.1 Central Question
    A.1.2 Theme Development
    A.1.3 Educational Objectives
    A.1.4 Communications
    A.1.5 Key Design Approaches and Exhibit Content Organization
    A.1.6 Key Outreach Components
    A.1.7 Planning Retreats

A.2 Research and Evaluation
    A.2.1 Research
        A.2.1.1 Surveys
        A.2.2.2 Related Product Review
        A.2.2.3 Subject Matter Experts
        A.2.2.4 Core Team/Extended Team

    A.2.2 Evaluation
        A.2.2.1 Front End Evaluation
        A.2.2.2 Community Groups Workshops
        A.2.2.3 Audience Definition
            A.2.2.3.1 Surveys
            A.2.2.3.2 Analysis
            A.2.2.3.3 Report
        A.2.2.4 Focus Groups

A.3 Statement of Purpose Report
    A.3.1 Initial Draft
    A.3.2 Redraft
    A.3.3 Extended Team Review Draft
    A.3.4 Approval Draft and Presentation
    A.3.5 Approved SOP Report

A.4 Development and Marketing
    A.4.1 Marketing Concept
    A.4.2 Fundraising Feasibility

A.5 Project Management
    A.5.1 Definition Phase
        A.5.1.1 Schedule and Budget Development and Tracking
        A.5.1.2 Core and Extended Team Organization Development
        A.5.1.3 Risk Management
            A.5.1.3.1 Project Risk Management
            A.5.1.3.2 Power, Influence, Authority (PIA) Analysis
        A.5.1.4 Project Reviews
            A.5.1.4.1 Project Progress
            A.5.1.4.2 Approval Review
        A.5.1.5 Project Reports

    A.5.2 Planning Phase
        A.5.2.1 WBS and Scope
        A.5.2.1 Resource, Schedule and Budget Development

continues

FIGURE 5-7   continued

```
        A.5.3  Other Phases
                A.5.3.1  Initial WBS and Scope
                A.5.3.2  Initial Resource, Schedule and Budget
                         Development

        A.5.4  Project Management Office
                A.5.4.1  Core and Extended Team
                A.5.4.2  Project Support Office
```

was developed as a team effort of the organization responsible for exhibit programs and was designed to be a template for future projects. Each phase in the program was planned as an independent project and each phase has its own WBS.

The project definition phase of the project lifecycle begins when the idea statement is approved and the go-ahead is received to define the project. The primary output of this project is an approved statement of purpose with supporting documents. Secondary outputs are WBS and scope descriptions, schedules, and budgets for the planning phase, and an initial WBS, scope statement, schedules, and budgets for the successor phases of the program.

This product-type project has cross-cutting analytical WBS elements in A.1, content and concept development, and A. 2, research and evaluation. The primary product is A.3, statement of purpose report, with secondary products of A.4, development and marketing, and A.5, project management. Chapter 3 discusses the work of the project management element, which includes normal project management work in A.5.1 and A.5.4 for this phase (project), but also includes work and deliverables for future phases in A.5.2 and A.5.3.

The numbering system deviates from the strictly numerical system discussed previously. Each phase (project) is assigned a letter prefix that is used with all elements in that phase.

> The WBS principles presented in this book apply universally to all kinds of projects, whether the output is a product, service, or results. If the work to be performed meets the definition of a project, then the WBS is a useful tool for managing the project.

NOTES

1. P. C. Dinsmore, "Enterprise Project Management: A Road Map for Getting Off to the Right Start," *PM Network* (June 2000), 27–31.
2. Ibid, p. 27.
3. C. Grove, W. Hallowell, and C. Smith, "A Parallel WBS for International Projects," *PM Network*® (March 1999), 37–42.

CHAPTER 6

WBS Principles, Steps, and Checklist

This chapter includes three parts that summarize the material presented in this book: (1) a set of WBS principles, (2) pragmatic steps for the project manager to follow in developing a WBS, and (3) a recommended checklist for the project manager to use in reviewing the WBS.

A checklist, like the WBS templates presented in the previous chapter, is not a substitute for thinking, and its use has some of the elements of *thinking inside the box*.

Figure 6-1 repeats the generic WBS of Chapter 2, but expands it to include additional information. The figure illustrates the different types of projects and their typical next level type of elements, as well as the different types of cross-cutting elements.

WBS PRINCIPLES

The following are sets of WBS principles, each of which has been discussed.

Top Level

- A program WBS includes a series of projects or lifecycle phases at Level 2 and also includes a program management element.
- The work breakdown under each phase (or project) of a program WBS is unique to the phase (or project) reflecting the deliverable to be produced at the end of the phase.
- Projects or phases of a program WBS have project management as an element at the first level decomposition.
- The WBS for a project is product-, service-, or results-oriented. The Level 2 breakdown will depend on the type.

Product Projects

- The Level 2 elements in a product project usually include the primary and any other major deliverables and major cross-cutting elements necessary to support the product work.

FIGURE 6-1   Generic Work Breakdown Structure Elements

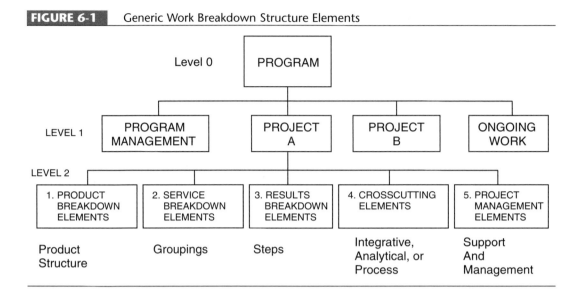

- The Level 3 elements of the product reflect the natural structure of the product.
- Cross-cutting elements are integrative, analytical, or process.

Service Projects

- The Level 2 WBS elements of a service project are the major areas where work is required to support the overall objectives of the project.
- The WBS elements in a service WBS are groupings of similar tasks, usually able to be assigned to one individual or organization.
- The WBS elements subdivide into areas or functions related to the parent category or grouping.
- A WBS for a new service project can be developed by looking for logical groupings of the tasks—a bottom-up approach.

Results Projects

- The Level 2 elements of a results project are standard process steps acknowledged to achieve the results.
- The Level 3 elements of a results project are usually standard process steps within the parent element.

Common Principles

- The WBS covers the total scope of the project. Work not in the WBS is not in the project.

- All deliverables or output products are represented in the WBS.
- The sum of the elements at each level represents 100 percent of the work of the next higher level. (The sum of the Level 2 items is 100 percent of the project work or cost.)
- Work in each element is equivalent to the sum of the work in the subordinate elements.
- The subdivisions should be logical and reflect the nature of the product, service, or result.
- Each WBS element should represent a discrete element of work that can be described in the WBS dictionary.
- Each WBS element should have a unique identifier.
- WBS element descriptors preferably should be nouns, with adjective modifiers if necessary. For clarity or for cultural reasons, WBS descriptors may include verbs and modifiers. However, they should not be considered activities since activities are by definition the action elements that occur below the WBS.
- The work in each WBS element may be described in detail in a WBS dictionary, which may become the basis for statements of work or work-authorizing documents.
- Project management is a Level 2 element in all WBSs.
- Stakeholders should participate in the development of the WBS.
- The WBS should be baselined after approval by the stakeholders.
- A formal change process should exist for baselined WBSs.
- The WBS should focus on project output or deliverables; it is not an organization chart, a schedule, or a resource list.
- The lowest level should be the level above the activities—the work package level.
- The lowest level should permit adequate control and visibility for project management.
- The lowest level need not be the same for all branches of the WBS.
- The lowest level should not be so detailed as to create an administrative burden.
- The WBS does not reflect time relationships or horizontal relationships between elements; all structural relationships are vertical.

STEPS IN DEVELOPING A WBS

The recommended steps to develop a WBS are as follows:

Step 1. Identify the project objectives. (This will assist in steps 2 and 3.)

Step 2. Determine the general type of project by identifying specifically whether the primary output is a product, service, or result.

Step 3A. If the project output is a product, Level 2 will include the product name, secondary product names, and cross-cutting elements. Make sure all project outputs can be related to a Level 2 element. (Proceed to step 4.)

Step 3B. If the project output is a service, Level 2 will include the top-level groupings of the various types of work and the project management element. Consider identifying as many activities as possible and grouping them by logical categories related to areas of work (bottom-up synthesis). (Proceed to step 5.)

Step 3C. If the project output is a result, Level 2 will consist of the major steps in the acknowledged process necessary to achieve the result plus the project management element. (Proceed to step 6.)

Step 4. For product WBSs, subdivide the product element into the logical physical breakdown of the product. Subdivide the cross-cutting elements into the supporting work. (Proceed to step 7.)

Step 5. For service WBSs, subdivide the Level 2 WBS elements into logical functional work areas. (Proceed to step 7.)

Step 6. For results WBSs, subdivide each Level 2 WBS elements into the standard processes specified to achieve the objective or output of the element. (Proceed to step 7.)

Step 7. Review the work at each level to make sure 100 percent of the work is identified; add elements as necessary. In a product WBS, make sure integrative elements are added as necessary.

Step 8. Continue to subdivide the elements to the work package level. Further subdivision would violate the principles outlined above. Stop when the next level would be activities or is unknown until further analysis or planning is performed.

Step 9. Review the WBS with stakeholders and adjust as necessary to make sure that all the project work is covered.

CHECKLIST

Figure 6-2 presents a checklist for the project team to use to evaluate the adequacy of the WBS.

FIGURE 6-2   WBS Checklist

❏   Have the project team and other stakeholders participated in the development of the WBS? Have the functional experts been involved?

❏   Does the WBS make sense from the point of view of how the organization does business?

❏   Is it clear from the descriptions of each element "what" work is to be done?

❏   Are all end products or deliverables identified clearly in the WBS?

❏   Is there a Project Management element at Level 2?

❏   Does the sum of the work represented by all the Level 2 elements add up to 100% of the work on the project (i.e., 100% of the scope)?

❏   Does the sum of the work represented by all the child elements under each parent element add up to 100% of the work of the parent?

❏   Have integrative elements been added where necessary to account for "assembly-type" of work?

❏   Do the work packages appear to be reasonable in size?

❏   Is the WBS element numbering logical and related to other organization numbering schemes, if possible?

❏   Do any parent elements represent organizations? If so, consider reworking that part of the WBS.

❏   If outsourcing or subcontracting are to be performed, is all the work to be contracted to a specific organization under a single, discrete element?

❏   Is the name of each element understandable in terms of what it represents or is a WBS dictionary required?

Think of the WBS simply as an outline of the work in the project and a tool to help approach the planning and scheduling one organized bite at a time.

Bibliography

Abramovici, Adrian. "Controlling Scope Creep." *PM Network* (January 2000): 44-48.

Berg, Cindy, and Kim Colenso. "Work Breakdown Structure Practice Standard Project—WBS vs. Activities." *PM Network* (April 2000): 69-71.

Central PERT Department, Product Programming, Orlando Division, *PERT TIME*, Martin Marietta, Document OR 3424, Vol. I, September 1963.

Dinsmore, Paul C. "Enterprise Project Management: A Road Map for Getting Off to the Right Start." *PM Network* (June 2000): 27-31.

Fleming, Quentin W. *Put Earned Value (C/SCSC) into Your Management Control System* (Worthington, OH: Publishing Horizons, Inc., 1983).

Grove, Cornelius, Willa Hallowell, and Cynthia Smith. "A Parallel WBS for International Projects." *PM Network* (March 1999): 37-42.

Haugan, Gregory T. *PERT* (Baltimore, MD: Martin Marietta Space Systems Division, 1962).

Keene, Michael L. *Effective Professional Writing* (Lexington, MA: D.C. Heath & Company, 1987).

Kerzner, Harold. *Project Management, A Systems Approach to Planning, Scheduling and Controlling.* 7th Ed. (New York: John Wiley & Sons, 2001).

Kotter, John P. *Leading Change* (Boston: Harvard Business School Press, 1996).

Malcolm, D.G., J.H. Roseboom, C.E.Clark, and W. Fazar. "Application of a Technique for Research and Development Program Evaluation." *Operations Research, the Journal of the Operations Research Society of America* 7, no. 5 (1959): 646-669.

Munson, Warren F. "A Controlled Experiment in PERTing Costs." POLARIS PROJECTION, GE Ordnance Department, November 1961.

National Aeronautics and Space Administration. *NASA PERT and Companion Cost System Handbook* (Washington, D.C.: Director of Management Reports, National Aeronautics and Space Administration, October 30, 1962).

Office of the Secretary of Defense, National Aeronautics and Space Administration, *DoD and NASA Guide, PERT/COST Systems Design* (June 1962).

Project Management Institute Standards Committee. *A Guide to the Project Management Body of Knowledge* (Upper Darby, PA: Project Management Institute, 2000).

Rad, Parvis F. "Advocating a Deliverable-Oriented Work Breakdown Structure." *Cost Engineering* (12 December 1999): 35-39.

Raz, Tzvi and Shlomo Globerson. "Effective Sizing and Content Definition of Work Packages." *Project Management Journal*® (December 1998): 17-23.

U.S. Department of Defense. MIL-STD-881 *Work Breakdown Structures for Defense Materiel Items* (Washington, D.C.: Headquarters, Air Force Systems Command, Directorate of Cost Analysis, 1 November 1968).

U.S. Government Coordinating Group. *PERT Implementation Manual (Draft Copy)*, August 1964.

Walker, Melissa. *Writing Research Papers* (New York: W.W. Norton & Company, 1984).

Index